The Boundary Waters Canoe Area Wilderness: Examining Changes in Use, Users, and Management Challenges

Robert G. Dvorak
Alan E. Watson
Neal Christensen
William T. Borrie
Ann Schwaller

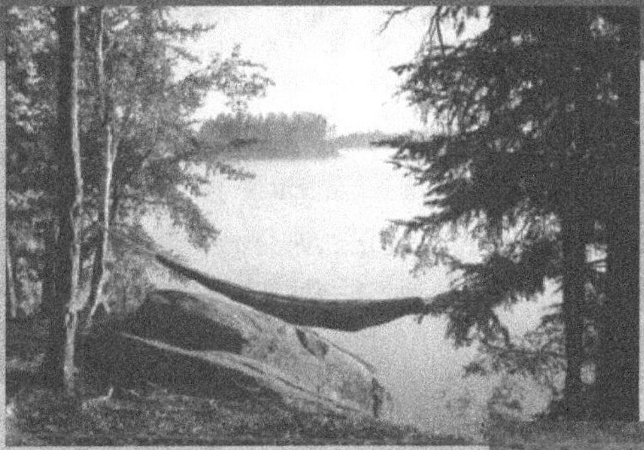

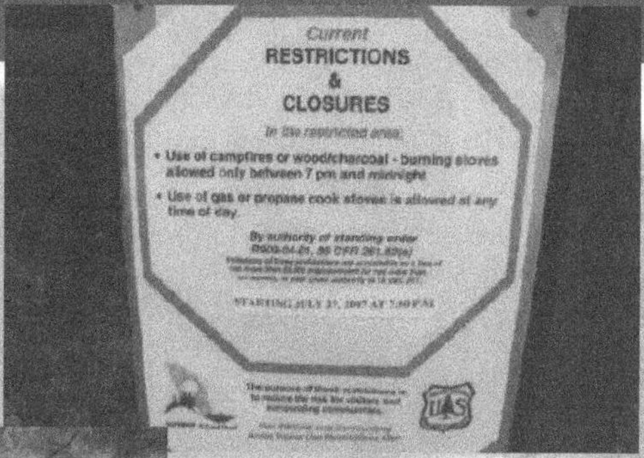

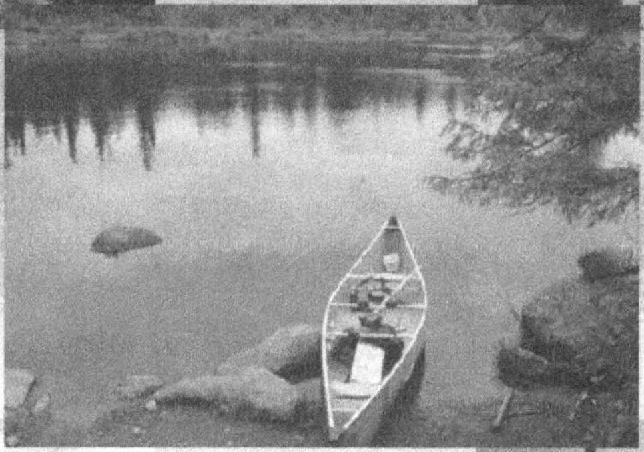

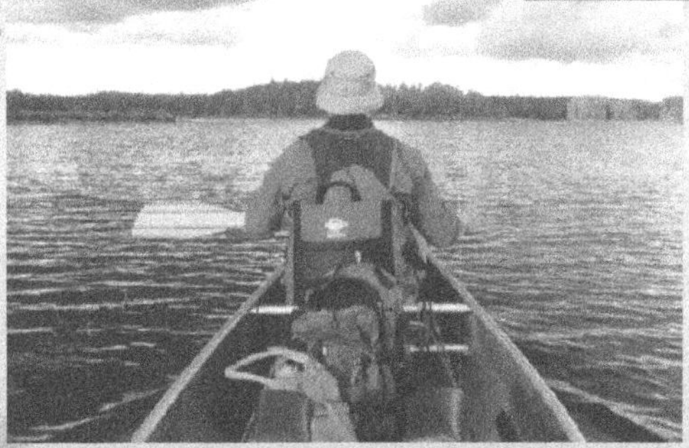

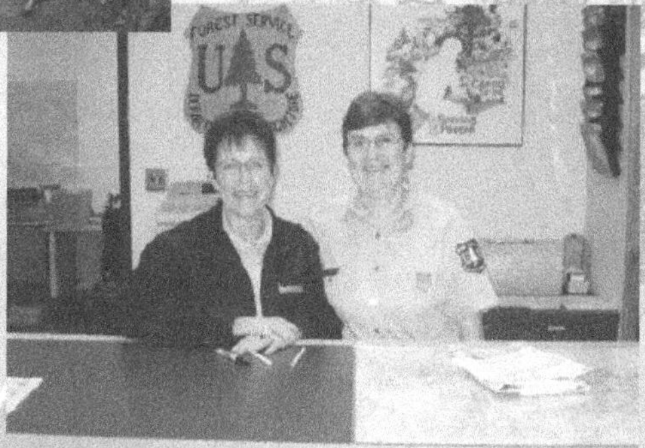

 United States Department of Agriculture / Forest Service

Rocky Mountain Research Station

Research Paper RMRS-RP-91

March 2012

Dvorak, Robert G.; Watson, Alan E.; Christensen, Neal; Borrie, William T.; Schwaller, Ann. 2012.
The Boundary Waters Canoe Area Wilderness: Examining changes in use, users, and management challenges. Res. Pap. RMRS-RP-91. Fort Collins, CO: U.S. Department of Agriculture, Forest Service, Rocky Mountain Research Station. 46 p.

Abstract

The purpose of this study was to determine trends in use and user characteristics at the Boundary Waters Canoe Area Wilderness. Based on data from 1969, 1991, and 2007, the average age of visitors has increased significantly, education levels have increased, and visitors remain predominantly male. Visitors in 2007 report seeing twice as many groups since 1961 and 1991, but the number of encounters are not exceeding expectations. Findings emerged related to gender ratios and evaluating resource conditions. These findings may need further investigation and future management action to provide opportunities for meaningful wilderness experiences while protecting wilderness character.

Keywords: wilderness users, user trends, experiences, encounters

Authors

Robert G. Dvorak, Assistant Professor, Central Michigan University, Mount Pleasant, MI, e-mail: dvora1rg@cmich.edu.

Alan E. Watson, Research Social Scientist, Aldo Leopold Wilderness Research Institute, USDA Forest Service, Rocky Mountain Research Station, Missoula, MT, e-mail: awatson@fs.fed.us.

Neal Christensen, Social Scientist, Christensen Research Company, Missoula, MT, e-mail: neal@ChristensenResearch.com.

William T. Borrie, Professor, University of Montana, Missoula, MT, e-mail: bill.borrie@umontana.edu.

Ann Schwaller, Natural Resource Wilderness Specialist, Superior National Forest, Duluth, MN, email: annschwaller@fs.fed.us.

*Cover photos: **Top left:** Lake 3 in July 2010 (photo by Robert Truax). **Top right:** Informational signage at entry point #30 Lake One during fire restrictions in the summer of 2007 (photo by Bob Dvorak). **Middle:** Lake Polly in 2007 (photo by Bob Dvorak). **Bottom left:** An approaching storm on Lake 4 in July 2010 (photo by Bob Dvorak). **Bottom right:** Superior National Forest staff at the Kawishiwi permit station (photo by Bob Dvorak).*

Table of Contents

The Boundary Waters Canoe Area Wilderness: Examining Changes in Use, Users, and Management Challenges

Robert G. Dvorak
Alan E. Watson
Neal Christensen
William T. Borrie
Ann Schwaller

Introduction

The Wilderness Act of 1964 directs that wilderness be managed to preserve natural conditions and to provide outstanding opportunities for solitude or a primitive and unconfined type of recreation. The "established statement of policy" of this Act also indicates that the National Wilderness Preservation System is to be administered for the use and enjoyment of the American people in such a manner as will leave these areas unimpaired for future use and enjoyment as wilderness. To meet these management goals, managers must adapt their programs to changes in the amount and type of use and resulting conditions from that use.

Unfortunately, we know little about trends in the characteristics, activities, and preferences of visitors to wilderness and other wild lands. We conduct wilderness research often with the intent that one study at one point in time will guide management of a single wilderness or provide input for wilderness management in the same region for many years. In only a few instances have data collected been replicated to increase understanding of how changes in visitors, attitudes, or management might inform revisions to management planning. For example, Lucas (1985) and Borrie and McCool (2007) provided results from repeat studies at the Bob Marshall Wilderness Complex in Montana. These studies, however, mostly represent only large western wilderness areas characterized by heavy stock, hunting, and fall use. Thus, it is difficult to draw conclusions about likely trends in other wilderness areas around the country based on repeat studies in Montana.

Cole and others (1995) combined findings from earlier repeat Bob Marshall Complex studies with coordinated repeat studies at the Desolation Wilderness in California, Shining Rock Wilderness in North Carolina, and the Boundary Waters Canoe Area Wilderness in Minnesota.

While these studies did include sites from the West, the South, and the Upper Midwest of the United States, there was no Alaska site available for a repeat study. They concluded that only 5 out of 83 wilderness use and user characteristics investigated changed consistently in these four wildernesses over time. These changes in use and user characteristics reflected that visitors were older, had achieved more education, the proportion of females increased, and the proportion of visitors who had been to other wildernesses was higher. Condition of litter in wilderness also consistently improved, but perhaps the most dramatic change was the decrease in wilderness participation by individuals under 25 years old. Some variables, such as previous experience in a specific wilderness and participation in hunting, increased substantially in some of these wildernesses but decreased substantially in others.

Cole and others (1995) suggest that, across time, the characteristics of people who visit wilderness have changed more than the types of trips they take, their evaluations of the conditions they encounter, or their preferences for conditions and management. Some evidence suggested that solo visitors were more common in the later studies and organized groups were less common. Groups seemed to be getting smaller and reported stays were shorter. All of these changes are subtle at best; in most cases, differences were not statistically significant.

Cole and others (1995) encouraged managers to be skeptical of broad generalizations about wilderness visitor trends that are occasionally advanced. Their findings suggest that little evidence exists to support the idea that the wilderness visitors of the 1990s or the trips they took were substantially different from those of a decade or two earlier. In the cases where there is a belief that important changes occur, change can only be accurately determined by conducting additional visitor studies specific to wildernesses of interest.

Baseline and trend studies of visitor use, impacts and preferences were conducted at the Boundary Waters Canoe Area Wilderness (BWCAW) in Minnesota in the 1960s and the 1990s. The information collected during these studies established objectives for visitor and resource management and developed wilderness and backcountry management strategies. A need existed, and an opportunity arose, to conduct an update on trends and current use information at the BWCAW. Managers need to know how visitors and their visits have changed to adapt management strategies to changing societal interests and needs.

The purpose of this research report is to examine trends in use and user characteristics at the Boundary Waters Canoe Area Wilderness (BWCAW) and to update knowledge about current visitors. While this report primarily focuses on trends analysis across two or three study points, this research also examined several issues not included in previous trends studies: the effects of recent wildfires, recreation visitor fees, and tree blowdown events on visits and visitors as well as day use.

Study Location

The Boundary Waters Canoe Area Wilderness is a 1,086,953-acre wilderness located on the Superior National Forest of northern Minnesota in the United States (USFS 2011). Comprising more than three million acres of land, water, and rock, the Superior National Forest spans 199 miles along the United States-Canadian Border and contains over 445,000 acres of surface water (USFS 2004). The BWCAW is a northern forest community of pine, fir, aspen, birch, sugar maple, and spruce trees and is home to numerous wildlife including deer, moose, beaver, gray wolves, otter, and black bear. This area has been highly visited for canoeing, camping and fishing for many years preceding Wilderness designation in 1964 (Figure 1).

The passage of the Wilderness Act in 1964 officially designated the BWCAW as part of the National Wilderness Preservation System. The BWCAW is the largest designated wilderness area east of the Mississippi River and is managed to retain its enduring value as wilderness and provide activities compatible with wilderness character (USFS 2004). In 1978, the Boundary Waters Canoe Area Wilderness Act added additional acreage to the wilderness, prohibited logging, created a mining protection area, and eliminated much of the motorized watercraft use (USFS 2004). This 1978 legislation also directed the Forest Service to establish quotas for motorboat use and to eliminate snowmobiling.

Previous BWCAW Research

Numerous wilderness recreation and resource management studies have been conducted in the BWCAW. These studies date back to at least the 1960s and include visitor impacts on newly developed campsites (Merriam and Smith 1974), studies to understand how visitors evaluate social conditions they encounter at the Boundary Waters Canoe Area Wilderness (Stankey 1973), investigations of perceptions of wilderness conditions related to previous experience (Watson and Cronin 1994), influences on opportunities for solitude (Watson 1995), and human response to large-scale natural disturbances (Lime 2000). Data from two of these previous studies are of particular interest and provide a basis to understand some trends in use and users at the Boundary Waters Canoe Area Wilderness.

1969 Visitor Use Study

George Stankey conducted the baseline visitor study for Boundary Waters visitors in 1969 (Stankey 1971) as a Ph.D. dissertation, which was included in a later Forest Service Research Publication (Stankey 1973). As a Forest Service scientist, Stankey studied visitors to three other areas, combining results for these three areas with results from the Boundary Waters Canoe Area into one report in 1973. With slightly less than 500 visitors contacted across the four areas, the initial sample for the BWCAW was only about 150 (73% response rate), all overnight users. However, while the dissertation presented very detailed information on BWCAW visitors, Stankey

Figure 1—The Boundary Waters Canoe Area was highly visited for canoeing, camping and fishing for many years preceding Wilderness designation in 1964.

(1973) focused mostly on perceptions of crowding and attitudes toward use level management across the four areas studied. While the 1969 study tended towards high use visitors and did not examine as many diverse issues as future studies, it still explored those issues most critical to management at that time.

1991 Trends Study

Cole and others (1995) examined trends in wilderness visitors and visits for the BWCAW in 1991, with a sample that attempted to replicate the methods of Stankey's 1969 study. The comparative 1991 sample included only those who entered through the same 14 moderate and heavy use portals sampled in 1969 (n = 215, 74% response rate). Data were collected from other portals, however, with a full data set of 295 (74% response rate) representing approximately 25% each from very high, high, moderate, and low use access points, extending beyond the data set used in the trends publication (Watson 1995; Watson and Cronn 1994). The intent of this full sample was to provide the best snapshot of all use, going beyond the purpose of the trend study to provide the most accurate picture of use as possible. Sampled permits were in proportion to actual use that occurred, trying to move away from over-representation of high use visitors as was apparent in the 1969 study. In both 1969 and 1991, collected data were only for overnight visitors as use was heavy and emphasis was on controlling resource and social impacts of the dominant, overnight use.

The Cole and others (1995) comparative analysis showed that many sociodemographic variables of BWCAW visitors changed significantly between 1969 and 1991. Specifically, the average age of respondents, higher achieved levels of education, and income had increased substantially. This is consistent with larger trends across other wilderness areas. However, gender proportions across samples remained the same, with the proportion of female visitors unchanged at just less than 30% (Cole and others 1995).The only significant change in visit characteristics between 1969 and 1991 was an increase in the proportion of groups that contained family members (1969 = 43%, 1991 = 53%). No changes in group type, group size and length of stay were significant. Changes also existed in perceptions of crowding reported between the 1969 and 1991 studies. More 1991 visitors felt the BWCAW was crowded in at least a few places (1969 = 31%, 1991 = 56%) (Cole and others 1995). Visitors in 1991 were also more likely to find it unpleasant to meet more than two paddle groups per day and increasing encounters affected them more negatively than 1969 visitors.

Methodology

The design for the 2007 trends study was informed by previous peer reviewed BWCAW studies conducted in 1969 and 1991 (Cole and others. 1995; Stankey 1971, 1973; Watson 1995) as well as by current knowledge about distribution of recreation use in the BWCAW, commitment to continually improve sampling methods, and input from Superior National Forest wilderness staff.

Sample Population

The population of interest for this study was current adult visitors (>15 years old) to the BWCAW during the peak season of May 1st to September 30th 2007. As of 2007, managers estimated total visitation per year at more than 250,000 visits (Figure 2). Permit data suggest that at least 130,000 day and multi-day visits occur during the peak period. For the 2007 study, an additional visitor population was sampled: day visitors. This supplemental sample developed primarily due to

Figure 2—In 2007, managers estimated total Boundary Waters Canoe Area Wilderness visitation at more than 250,000 visits per year.

manager perceptions that day use has changed and that a better understanding of day use patterns and day visitors themselves was necessary.

Sampling

The 1969 visitor sample (n = 152,73% response rate) resulted from contacts on-site as they finished their BWCAW trips and were asked to either complete a questionnaire at that time or provide contact information for later mailing of a questionnaire (see Stankey 1971, 1973). The 1991 study obtained over 200 usable surveys at the busiest entry points. Central permit distribution locations targeted lower use sites for a total sample of 295 (74% response rate) (see Watson 1995). Visitors completed a short on-site interview to collect information on a front-end form for later mailing of a post trip questionnaire.

Sampling from 1991 informed the 2007 sampling design. However, allocated permit data[1] and self-issue permit data were examined to represent the population more accurately. 2006 permit data suggested a difference in permit allocation based on both month and entry point (Pearson's χ^2=361.309, df= 64, p<.001). That is, permits were not uniformly issued by month or entry point, and thus a sampling design using only entry points could potentially lead to oversampling. Thus, sampling days were stratified simultaneously across both entry points and months during the peak season to account for this relationship. Seventy-six sample days were selected, which accounted for 50% of the days during the 142-day peak season.

The proportion of day and overnight use across all entry points was also determined using visitor population estimates. Day use was estimated using 2004 self-issue permit data for day visitor paddlers[2] and 2006 permit data for day visitor motorists. Overnight use was estimated only using 2006 allocated permit data (which included both motorized and non-motorized use). Based on these data, estimated overnight use accounted for 60% of total use, while day use accounted for 40%. These proportions were used to weight the primary sampling schedule.

Because random sampling at each of the 74 entry points (Figure 3) was logistically and practically impossible,

---

[1] Not all permits are redeemed, but it is assumed actual use is in proportion to allocated permits

[2] Self-issue permit data for 2005-2006 was not yet available.

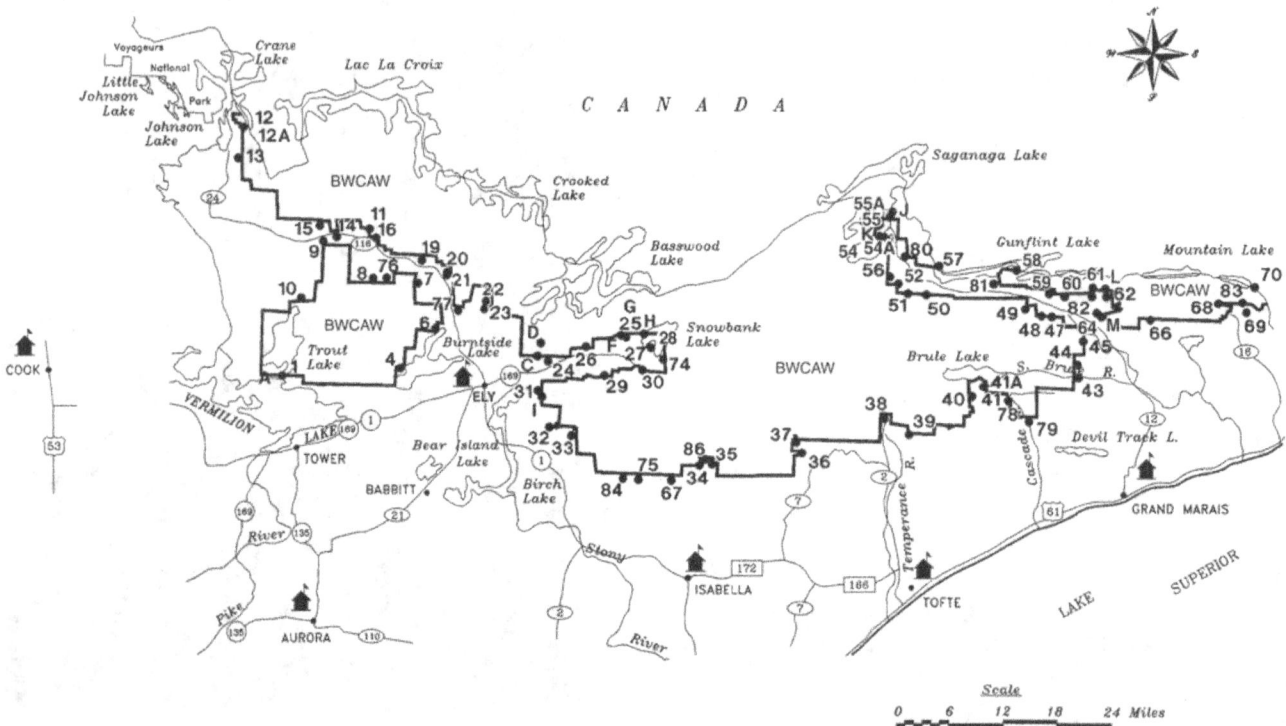

Figure 3—Map of Boundary Waters Canoe Area Wilderness and entry points (retrieved June 17, 2008 from http://www.fs.fed.us/r9/forests/superior/bwcaw/documents/EPMap.pdf).

the developed on-site sampling schedule included the busiest 17 entry/exit points. These points account for more than 70% of the total use during the peak season. Table 1 shows the 17 entry points sampled along with estimates of their types and levels of use during the peak season. Numbers preceding entry point names (e.g., 25-Moose Lake) represent their location on the map in Figure 3.

Sampling at entry points was for half days, alternating between entry hours (7:30-11:30 a.m.) and exit hours of the day (3-7 p.m.). The other half day was used to sample visitors prior to entry at overnight permit distribution centers, also known as permit issuing stations, alternating between opening (7-11 a.m.) and closing business hours (1-5 p.m.). This method was the most efficient for reaching overnight visitors who used low use entry points (as well as to contact visitors who launched from private sites not otherwise sampled). Four centralized communities, each having both Forest Service and private cooperator permit distribution, were used for centralized sampling (Table 2). The centralized location closest to the primary entry point for that day was used during the alternate half days.

On-Site Interview and Mailings

The primary purpose of the on-site interview was to collect contact information from all visitors in the group who were over 15 years of age so that they could be mailed a survey after they returned home from their trip (Figure 4). The secondary purpose was to provide an opportunity to make face-to-face contact with potential respondents and reinforce the importance of the research to them. Separate questionnaire formats were mailed to visitors, depending upon the type of trip they were on when contacted, overnight or day use.

Table 1—Visitor population estimates for Top 17 entry points.

Entry point	Over-night 2006	Day use motor 2006	Day use paddle 2004	Day use hike 2004	Total people	% of total visits	Cum %
						- - - - - percent- - - - -	
25-Moose Lake	9,196	8,300	3,263		20,759	16	16
24-Fall Lake	3,938	5,895	1,027		10,860	9	25
55-Saganaga Lake	3,722	5,344	454	22	9,543	8	33
30-Lake One	8,200		1,085		9,285	7	40
38-Sawbill Lake	4,831		1,584		6,415	5	45
27-Snowbank Lake	3,151	401	376		3,928	3	48
01-Trout Lake	2,143	1,710	18		3,872	3	51
54-Seagull Lake	2,215	143	808		3,166	3	54
79-Eagle Mountain	32		0	2,972	3,004	2	56
16-Moose River	2,916		76		2,992	2	58
60-Duncan Lake	1,112		994	884	2,990	2	61
37-Kawishiwi Lake	2,576		275		2,851	2	63
23-Mudro Lake	2,530		267		2,797	2	65
41-Brule Lake	2,323		372	12	2,707	2	67
14-L. Indian Sioux	2,495		198		2,693	2	69
77-South Hegman	567		1,873	71	2,511	2	71
31-From Farm Lake	1,042		1,184	47	2,273	2	73

Table 2—Permit distribution locations.

Town	Ranger District	# of Sample days
Cook, MN	La Croix	7
Ely, MN	Kawishiwi	43
Tofte, MN	Tofte	9
Grand Marais, MN	Gunflint	16

Figure 4—In 2007, a sample of BWCAW visitors were contacted to update knowledge about use and user characteristics.

Approximately 2 weeks after the onsite interview, a survey packet was mailed to individuals. Packets included a cover letter describing the study in detail, a questionnaire to be completed, and a pre-paid envelope to return the questionnaire. Packet mailings followed a modified Dillman (2007) approach, with a reminder/thank you postcard sent 1 week after the first mailing and a replacement questionnaire and letter sent 2 weeks after the postcard. Any undeliverable or duplicate packets were noted and removed from future mailings.

Response Rates and Non-response Bias

A total of 811 questionnaires were returned, for a 67.6% overall response rate (Table 3). After adjusting for unusable questionnaires, the sample consisted of 613 overnight and 186 day use completed questionnaires. Non-response checks were performed on the overnight and day use samples to investigate any possible bias between respondents and non-respondents. The variables of comparison were *Number of Previous Visits to the BWCAW* and *Year of 1ˢᵗ Visit*. Across the samples, results from independent sample t-tests suggest no significant differences between respondents and non-respondents for *Number of Previous Visits to the BWCAW* at $p = 0.05$. However, significant differences were present between non-respondents and respondents for *Year of 1ˢᵗ Visit* in the overnight respondents (Table 4). Closer

examination of this difference represents a mean difference of 4-5 years, biasing the sample toward an earlier year of first visit for respondents. First-time BWCAW users also represented the largest category (16%) for the *Year of 1ˢᵗ Visit* variable in the overnight respondents. Additionally weighting the sample toward first-time visitors would be overemphasizing an already substantial segment and inappropriate. Thus, differences were not interpreted to be practically significant.

Table 3—Distribution and response rates of questionnaires[a].

Questionnaire format	Distributed	Returned	Response rate
Overnight	903	613	69.2%
Day use	296	186	67.1%
Total	1,199	811	67.6%

[a] Response rates adjusted for undeliverable mailings.

Table 4—Significant differences for Year of 1st Visit.

Overnight questionnaire	Mean year	Std. dev (in years)	t-value
Respondents (n = 602)	1990	14.163	-4.689
Non-respondents (n = 285)	1994	13.029	$P < 0.001$

Results

The following section describes the trends analysis results from the data collected for the overnight questionnaires. Results are presented first for those items with data from 1969, 1991, and 2007. Then, items with only 1991 and 2007 data are presented. Lastly, day visitor respondent data for these same variables are presented.

It is important that overnight and day use results **should not** be directly compared to one another. While the sample of overnight respondents is arguably representative of overnight visitors during the 2007 peak season, the sample of day visitor respondents is not. Examination of recent permit data suggests day use accounts for approximately 40% of all BWCAW use. While the 186 day visitor questionnaires provide new insight into this type of BWCAW use not previously examined, it is not appropriate to generalize the day use results to all day visitors of the BWCAW.

It is also important that the reader should consider both statistically significant differences and practical significance when examining results. Statistical significance and the effect size of differences are sensitive to sample size. A limitation of this study is the proportionate differences in sample size across years. Thus, relatively small differences may be statistically significant, but represent less practical significance. These are important points for consideration when interpreting results.

Finally, 95% confidence intervals are provided in the results, where applicable[3]. These intervals are interpreted such that with 95% confidence, the means and percentages reported are within the ranges given.

1969-1991-2007 Trends Analysis

Visitor Demographics—Respondents were asked several questions in the mail-back questionnaire that were included to provide trends in demographic characteristics of overnight visitors to the BWCAW across all three data sets: education, proportion of students, gender, membership in environmental/outdoor recreation organizations, and visitors' past wilderness experience.

Age—Respondents reported their age on their last birthday. While the 1969 sample reported an average age of 26, and the average age in 1991 had increased to 36, in 2007 this average had increased further to 45 (Table 5). About two-thirds of overnight visitors in 2007 described themselves as being 40 years of age or older.

Education—Respondents reported their highest attained level of education (Table 6). Approximately 73% of overnight respondents in 2007 had attained at least

---

[3] For questions with multiple response categories (e.g. family, friends, alone), confidence intervals cannot be easily calculated

Table 5—Sociodemographic characteristics of overnight visitors.

Year	Mean age	Med. education	Students %	Females %	Conserv. Org %
1969	26 (±1.5)	12	47 (±6.0%)	25 (±5.2%)	12 (±3.9%)
1991	36 (±1.3)	16	18 (±3.7%)	30 (±4.4%)	35 (±4.6%)
2007	45 (±1.1)	16	11 (±2.4%)	25 (±3.5%)	29 (±3.6%)
Significance	*<0.001*	*<0.001*	*<0.001*	*0.22*	*<0.001*

Table 6—Percentage of overnight visitors for education levels.

Year	Not high school grad	High school grad	Some college	College grad	Grad study	Median (years)
			- - - - percent - - - -			
1969	20	31	29	5	15	12
1991	0	16	24	16	44	16
2007	1	5	20	33	40	16

an undergraduate college degree. Further, a large portion of respondents reported having attended graduate school, with 33% of overnight visitors having completed a graduate degree. Only about 1% had completed less education than a high school diploma. Respondents reported if they currently were a student at the time of their visit (Table 5). Trends are toward fewer students in the BWCAW. While the sample in 1969 (age 16 or older) were almost half students (47%), this proportion dropped to less than one-fifth (18%) in 1991 and dropped further to only about one-tenth of the sample (11%) by 2007.

While overall education attainment medians seem to have risen between 1969 (12 years) and 1991 (16 years) and then remained stable (Table 5), more specific examination shows a substantial increase in college graduates in 2007 (Table 6). This proportion increased from 5% in 1969 to 16% in 1991 and to 33% in 2007. This change accompanies a change from 20% to 1% of visitors reporting not graduating from high school.

Gender—Nearly three-quarters of surveyed overnight visitors in 2007 were male (Table 5). While this number is high, it has not increased significantly. The proportion of females appears to have remained stable at the BWCAW over time, with fluctuation over the past 40 years remaining between 25 and 30 percent of the overnight visitors.

Membership in Outdoor Recreation or Conservation Organizations—From 1969 to 1991, there

were dramatic increases in the proportion of visitors who reported being members of outdoor recreation or conservation organizations. This proportion increased from 12% of visitors who reported such memberships in 1969, to 35% in 1991. However, this trend did not continue to 2007. The 2007 sample reported a slight, but significant reduction to 29% of the visitors holding such memberships. In 2007, the most common organizations listed were the National Audubon Society, Sierra Club, Nature Conservancy, Boy Scouts of America, Ducks Unlimited, and the Friends of the Boundary Waters.

Previous Wilderness Experience—While nearly one-third of visitors in 1969 were on their first trip to the BWCAW, this number dropped to 12% in 1991 and dropped further to only 6% in 2007 (Table 7). In 2007, overnight visitors reported an average of roughly 12 previous visits to the BWCAW. Just less than half of the visitors in 1969 had visited other wildernesses besides the BWCAW at that time, but this rose to 57% by 1991 and 75% by 2007 (Table 7).

Frequency of Wilderness Trips—About 68% of overnight visitors reported taking a wilderness trip at least once a year in 2007. Visitors in 1991 reported similar numbers, with also about 67% taking wilderness trips at least once per year. In 1969, the reported number was 67% (Table 8). However, the proportion taking more than one wilderness trip per year decreased significantly from 44% in 1969 to 34% in 1991 and further decreased to 31% in 2007 (Table 8).

Table 7—Percentage of overnight visitors with previous wilderness experience.

Wilderness experience	1969	1991	2007	Significance	Test
First time to BWCAW	30 (±5.5%)	12 (±3.1%)	6 (±1.8%)	<0.001	X^2
Experience in other wildernesses	47 (±7.1%)	57 (±4.8%)	75 (±3.5%)	<0.001	X^2

Table 8—Percentage of overnight visitors indicating typical wilderness visitation.

	Wilderness trip frequency			
Year	Less than once every 2 years	About once every 2 years	About once per year	More than once per year
	----------------------- percent -----------------------			
1969	25	8	23	44
1991	15	18	33	34
2007	22	10	37	31
	X^2, p<0.001			

Trip Characteristics—There were also variables in all three studies that described the visitor's trip. These included group size and group composition, the length of overnight trips, number of people they saw while they traveled or camped, and reporting of crowded conditions.

Group Size and Composition—In 1969 the average group size was 5.2 people per party, by 1991 it had dropped to 4.5 and decreased only slightly to 4.4 by 2007 (Table 9). Between the 1991 and 2007 studies, the party size limit reduced from 10 persons to 9. Though there are groups that meet the maximum size limit of nine people and four boats, they do not dominate use. While the average group size has decreased over the three studies, possibly due to changes in group size limits, the trend has also been for more solo trips, though numbers of solo visitors remains very low and no significant increase was found at the BWCAW since 1991 (Table 9).

Groups in 2007 were more likely to describe themselves as composed of family members (68.7%) than in 1969 and 1991, when less than half described their groups that way (Table 9). Only 5.1% of overnight groups described themselves as an organization or club in 2007, a significant decrease from 1991 (9.9%) and 1969 (11.1%).

Length of Overnight Trips—The average length of stay for overnight visitors increased over the time of these studies (Table 9). While the change is not large, a consistent, significant trend from 4.0 nights in 1969 to 4.2 nights in 1991 and to 4.4 nights in 2007 was evident ($p = 0.035$).

Number of Groups Seen—Respondents in all three studies estimated the number of other groups they saw during their trip (Table 10). The total number of groups they reported was divided by the number of days of their trip as an average estimate of social conditions they found on their trips. No difference was reported between 1969 (4.1 groups seen per day) and 1991 (4.2 groups seen per day); however, the number more than doubled by 2007 to 8.6 groups per day.

Visitors also reported the number of large groups they saw during their trip. This number also increased dramatically from 1969, when the average per day was only about one-half of a group (or one group every other day). By 2007, this number increased to 4.2 groups on average per day. The definitions also changed over the years due to changes in group size limits. A large group in 1969 was defined as more than nine members, in 1991, it was more than 10 people and in 2007, it was not defined.

Table 9—Summary statistics of overnight visitors on trip characteristics.

Visit characteristics	1969	1991	2007	Significance	Test
Solo visitors (%)	0.5	1.9	2.3	0.17	x^2
Organized groups (%)	11.1	9.9	5.1	0.002	x^2
Groups with family members (%)	43.3	47.6	68.7	<0.001	x^2
Mean group size (people)	5.2	4.5	4.4		
	(±0.69)	(±0.29)	(±0.17)	0.003	ANOVA
Mean length of stay (nights)	4.0	4.2	4.4		
	(±0.39)	(±0.22)	(±0.15)	0.035	ANOVA

Table 10—Summary statistics of overnight visitors for social conditions.

Social condition	1969	1991	2007	Significance
Mean number of other groups/day	4.1	4.2	8.6	0.002
Mean number of large groups/day[a]	0.5	0.1	4.2	

[a] Large groups defined as: 1969: >9; 1991: >10; 2007: not defined.

Crowding Perceptions—Respondents reported whether they felt the BWCAW was too crowded (Table 11). A significant change in response to this question was found, with fewer than 40% saying they *did not* experience crowded conditions in 2007, decreasing from 44% in 1991 and from 72% in 1969. Over half felt it was crowded in at least a few places in 2007, a big change from 1969 when only 24% reported crowding in at least a few places. Consistently, fewer than 10% in all three studies reporting crowding in most places they visited on their trips, though it went up from 2% in 1969 to 9% in 2007. Of the individuals who felt it was crowded at least in some places in 2007, 81% were either a little or moderately bothered by the amount of people (compared to 56% in 1991 and 84% in 1969). Only 12% were bothered a lot in 2007. Only 2% reported in 2007 that they changed the length of their trip due to crowding, while 17% changed the route of their trip. Finally, 28% of all overnight visitors in 2007 reported crowding would affect their plans to visit the BWCAW.

1991-2007 Trends Analysis

In 1991, it was apparent that there were additional issues that needed to be included in a survey of visitors that managers wanted to know about but were not included in the 1969 study. This was because the 1969 study was for a purpose other than solely establishing a baseline for comparison and tracking trends. Therefore, additional questions were added in 1991 to describe better the trip, what visitors encountered there, and how they evaluated what they found. The 2007 survey obtained responses to many of these questions first asked in 1991 to allow analysis of change across at least these two points in time. A small number of additional demographic questions were included in both studies, but some are difficult to compare due to changing categories of responses.

First, race or ethnicity was included in 1991 and 2007, but not in 1969. Very simply, in both years the responding visitors were about 97% white, with very low numbers indicating Hispanic origin. Similarly, there was very low representation of American Indian or Alaska Native, Asian and Pacific Islander. No African American respondents completed surveys in either 1991 or 2007. The second question difficult to compare across studies was actually in all three surveys: household income. Response categories at the time of each study corresponded closely to categories used in U.S. Census surveys; those changed, making comparisons difficult. However, in 1990 dollars, a median income can be estimated to have changed from $31,500 in 1969 to $43,000 in 1991 and to $44,000 in 2007. Nearly half of current overnight visitors described their annual household income as ranging from $60,000 to $120,000 in 2007 dollars. Approximately 6% of overnight visitors described their income as less than $20,000 annually.

One more demographic question introduced in 1991 and repeated in 2007 was about the type of residence of visitors (type of community they live in now) and where they grew up (to age 18). The trend from these data (Table 12) indicate that visitors today at the BWCAW are about half as likely to have grown up on a farm, much more likely to have grown up in a major city or metro area and are also more likely to live in a major city or metro area of over 1 million people.

Trip Features—Particular features of the trip were examined in 1991 and 2007. These included the method of travel on the trip, participation in fishing, and use of fuel for cooking and woodfires.

Table 11—Percentage of overnight visitors indicating crowding opinions.

Visitor opinion	1969	1991	2007
	------- percent -------		
Not overcrowded	72	44	38
Crowded in a few places	24	47	51
Crowded in most places	2	8	9
Did not notice	2	2	2
$X^2 p < 0.0001$			

Table 12—Percentage of overnight visitors current and childhood place of residence.

Type of community	Childhood		Current	
	1991	2007	1991	2007
	---------- percent ----------			
Agricultural farm/ranch	24.1	12.2	5.8	3.9
Rural or small town	11.2	14.4	13.6	17.1
Town, large village (1,000-5,000)	26.1	11.7	6.9	8.8
Small city (5,000-50,000)	13.2	27.2	19.6	25.8
Medium city (50,000- 1 million)	25.4	18.3	22.0	21.5
Major city or metro area (over 1 million)	0	16.2	12.7	23.0

Method of Travel—While our samples included different proportions of visitors who reported using private non-motorized boats for their trips, (72% in 1991 and 68% in 2007), this did not represent a significant shift in method of travel. The increase from 18% renting non-motorized boats in 1991 to 26% in 2007, however, was a significant increase (Table 13). Less than 40% of overnight visitors in 2007 used the services or purchased supplies from an outfitter. Only 6% of overnight groups describe themselves as fully outfitted. Our sample also included a much lower proportion of private motorized users in 2007 (5%) than our sample in 1991 (11%).

Participation in Fishing—Fishing is a major activity in the BWCAW. While not an exclusive BWCAW wilderness value, it is a common activity of engagement and a big part of experiences there. We asked two questions about fishing in 1991 and 2007 in order to follow some trends in engagement and the role of fishing in trips there. From 1991 to 2007, the reported proportion of respondents who fished during their trip dropped from 83% to 77%. This was a significant change (Table 14). We also asked them if they fished, whether it was a priority for the trip. Of those that fished, there was also a significant decrease in the importance they attached to it (47% described the fishing as a major reason for going on the trip in 1991, 35% in 2007).

Use of Fuel for Cooking and Woodfires—With substantial concern about woodfire resource impacts in BWCAW campsites, a set of questions in 1991 was introduced to document the type of reported fuels used for cooking and frequency of woodfires for other purposes than cooking. The proportion of visitors who use gas stoves for cooking drastically increased from 1991 to 2007 (63% to 91%) (Figure 5, Table 14). The number of cooking fires correspondingly decreased and the number of evening fires that were not for cooking but instead for sitting around and enjoying, decreased from nearly 2 on average per trip to closer to 1 (Table 14).

Inter-group Encounters—Most items studied in 1991 and 2007 concerned what the visitors encountered on their trips and their evaluations of what they encountered. These included encounter levels, how encounters matched their expectations for encounters, problems potentially needing management attention, and evaluations of "general" wear and tear on the resource.

Table 13—Percentage of overnight visitors indicating method of travel.

Method of travel	1991	2007	Significance	Test
Private non-motorized	72	68		
	(±5.2%)	(±3.7%)	0.264	t-test
Rented non-motorized	18	26		
	(±4.3%)	(±3.5%)	0.0057	t-test
Private motorboat	11	5		
	(±3.6%)	(±1.7%)	0.0024	t-test

Table 14—Percentage of overnight visitors indicating trip features.

Trip feature	1991	2007	Significance	Test
Fished	83	77	0.024	t-test
	(±4.7%)	(±3.3%)		
Fishing a priority	47	35	<0.001	t-test
	(±6.3%)	(±3.8%)		
Used gas stove	63	91	<0.001	t-test
	(±5.6%)	(±2.2%)		
Number of cook fires	3.5	1.7	<0.001	t-test
	(±.43)	(±.26)		
Number of evening fires for enjoyment	1.8	1.4	0.004	t-test
	(±.24)	(±.16)		

Figure 5—The proportion of visitors who use gas stoves for cooking drastically increased from 1991 to 2007 (63% to 91%).

Encounter Levels—From 1991 to 2007, visitors reported seeing significantly more groups that camped within sight or sound of their own campsites and more groups traveling past within sight or sound of their campsites (Table 15). This last encounter element more than doubled from 4.8 for the trip in 1991 to 11.3 in 2007. The number of groups that were camped within sight or sound of their campsites increased less dramatically, but still significantly.

Visitors were also asked, in both years, to estimate the minimum number of groups they saw from their campsites and traveling past their campsite, within sight or sound. Mixed results were reported, with numbers doubling for encounters with people traveling past their campsites (from 0.9 in 1991 to 1.8 in 2007). The least number of groups that camped within sight or sound of their campsite in 1991 was not significantly different from that reported in 2007, on average (1991,0.6; 2007, 0.5) (Table 15).

Expectations for Encounters—Interestingly, although all measures of encounters included in both 1991 and 2007 indicated that encounters with other visitors increased in all aspects, visitor evaluations of these encounters did not vary substantially across years (Table 16) though the minority tended to report these encounter rates were less than they expected. Nearly half consistently reported they encountered about what they expected to encounter.

Resource Impacts Issues—Visitors in 1991 and 2007 indicated whether 19 different resource impact issues were a problem on their visit. Nine of these conditions seemed to improve (with a significantly lower proportion of the sample reporting it as a problem), one was worse, and nine stayed the same (Table 17). Notable among these trends was that seeing large numbers of people was the only potential problem that increased (from 13.3% in 1991 to 21.1% in 2007) in numbers of people indicating it was a problem for them during their trip. Evaluations of portage maintenance, litter, publicizing rules and regulations, advertising the permit requirement, obtaining permits, finding firewood, improper disposal of fish entrails, finding fire grates full of trash, and finding an unoccupied campsite were all substantially less problems in 2007 than 1991 (Table 17). Despite these trends, however, the largest problems reported in 2007 were too many people in the area (32.6%), getting information to help visitors avoid congested areas (27.4%), litter (27.3%) and finding an unoccupied campsite (25.6%).

Table 15—Summary statistics of overnight visitors inter-group encounters at campsites.

Encounter type	1991	2007	Significance	Test
Least camped in sight/sound per day	.6 (±.12)	.5 (±.07)	0.9035	t-test
Most camped in sight/sound per day	1.2 (±.15)	1.4 (±.11)	0.0959	t-test
Total trip camped in sight/sound	1.8 (±.27)	2.3 (±.25)	0.0195	t-test
Least boated in sight/sound per day	.9 (±.25)	1.8 (±.19)	<0.001	t-test
Most boated in sight/sound per day	2.5 (±.41)	5.4 (±.45)	<0.001	t-test
Total trip boated in sight/sound	4.8 (±.88)	11.3 (±1.0)	<0.001	t-test

Table 16—Percentage of overnight visitors indicating expectations for seeing groups.

Type of group encountered		Far fewer	Fewer	About what expected	More	Far more	No expectation
		- percent -					
Non-motorized groups	1991	3.0	15.3	45.1	24.1	10.5	2.0
	2007	1.3	9.0	52.7	23.4	11.1	2.5
Groups camped in sight/sound	1991	8.5	13.3	50.9	19.1	4.1	4.1
	2007	4.3	17.3	59.7	13.0	2.8	2.8
Groups floating in sight/sound	1991	5.8	17.4	46.4	18.8	6.5	5.1
	2007	2.3	15.2	53.1	19.9	7.7	1.8

Table 17—Percentage of overnight visitors indicating evaluation of conditions.

Problem	Not a problem		A problem		
	1991	2007	1991	2007	Significance
	- - - - - - - - - - - - - - - - - - percent - - - - - - - - - - - - - - - - - - -				
Portages poorly maintained	86.2	94.9	13.8	5.5	<0.001
Litter	61.2	72.7	38.8	27.3	<0.001
Inadequate disposal of human body waste	93.5	92.4	6.6	7.6	0.5581
Large groups of people	86.7	78.9	13.3	21.1	0.0029
Too many people in area	68.2	67.5	31.8	32.6	0.8269
Area rule/regulations not adequately publicized	83.4	91.9	16.6	8.1	<0.001
Not enough information on where other users like to be	73.1	72.6	26.9	27.4	0.8831
Permit requirement not well advertised	88.2	96.5	11.8	3.5	<0.001
Process of obtaining permit too difficult	89.0	93.3	11.0	6.7	0.0456
Not enough parking spaces at wilderness entry points	91.0	93.3	9.0	6.7	0.2301
Not enough firewood	75.5	87.9	24.5	12.1	<0.001
Too many day users	86.4	90.1	13.6	9.9	0.1148
Improper disposal of fish entrails	78.8	89.1	21.3	10.9	<0.001
Low flying aircraft	88.6	86.0	11.4	14.0	0.2908
Too many rules/regulations	92.4	94.0	7.6	6.0	0.3875
People making noise	83.7	84.1	16.3	15.9	0.8861
Fire grates full of charcoal/ash	83.4	87.5	16.6	12.5	0.1093
Fire grate full of trash	68.4	83.3	31.6	16.7	<0.001
Finding an unoccupied campsite	67.4	74.4	32.6	25.6	0.0294

Evaluations of Wear and Tear—Generally, visitor evaluations of resource conditions through a broad evaluation of wear and tear (erosion and loss of vegetation) and littering inside the BWCAW had little change. The majority of visitors in both 1991 and 2007 indicated they thought wear and tear conditions were good or very good. Evaluations of litter did improve slightly from about 55% in 1991 to 69% feeling it was good or very good in 2007 (Table 18).

New Issues Researched in 2007

An additional purpose of this research was to understand several new issues that had arisen since the previous studies. This included new issues related to wilderness permits, the introduction of user fees, and several natural disturbances such as the 1999 blowdown storm and recent wildfires. The following sections describe the attitudes and evaluations of overnight visitors for these specific issues.

Wilderness Permits—Permits are required year-round for all overnight visitors to the BWCAW. From May 1 to September 30, these permits are regulated through a quota system that manages the number of groups at each entry point per day. Each year, quota permits are obtained first via lottery. Applications are taken from December of the previous year until February and then allocated. Following the lottery, a first-come, first-served reservation process begins via website or phone. Finally, remaining quota permits can be obtained during the peak season on a walk-up basis from Forest Service and cooperator permit stations.

Overnight visitors answered questions on various aspects of the permit system at the BWCAW. This included if permits were reserved, if respondents applied for the lottery, if reservations were made online, and if a confirmation of the reservation was received (Table 19). Permits were reserved by over 95% of overnight visitors.

However, 30% of overnight visitors reported that someone else in their group was responsible for reserving the permit. Only 17% of overnight visitors used the lottery to reserve their permits. For those that did, visitors found it relatively easy to use. In contrast with the lottery, 62% of overnight visitors used the online reservation system to reserve their permit. Again overnight visitors found it relatively easy to use. Confirmations of permit reservations were received by 90% of overnight visitors.

Overnight visitors answered specific questions about picking up their permit. Over 78% of overnight respondents picked up their permits at Forest Service stations and approximately 22% at cooperator permit stations. These respondents were asked about the convenience of location and hours of operation for permit stations (Figure 6). Approximately 95% of respondents agreed or strongly agreed that the location was convenient. Nearly 87% agreed or strongly agreed that the hours of operation were convenient. Finally, overnight visitors answered if permit requirements were well advertised or if the process of obtaining a permit was too difficult. Over 96% of overnight visitors felt advertising was not a problem and 93% felt the process was not too difficult (Table 17). Approximately 4% of overnight visitors thought advertising was a problem and 7% felt the process was too difficult. However, these percentages decreased from 1991 and represent statistically significant changes.

User Fees—Overnight visitors answered questions regarding the fee program at the BWCAW (Table 20). Respondents were overwhelmingly supportive of different aspects of the fee program. This included the amount of the fee deposit (90% agreement), amount of reservations fees (87% agreement), overnight use fees (86% agreement), and the process of paying fees (94% agreement). The largest amount of disagreement related to the amount of the reservation fee (9%) and the amount of overnight use fees (10%). In addition, nearly 84% of overnight respondents agreed the BWCAW was better off due to fees (Figure 7).

Table 18—Percentage of overnight visitors indicating evaluation of wear and tear.

Conditions		Very good	Good	Fair	Poor	Very poor
		- - - - - - - - - - - - - - - - - *percent* - - - - - - - - - - - - - - - - -				
Wear and tear of conditions	1991	25.0	43.2	19.9	7.5	4.5
	2007	28.2	44.2	22.5	4.2	1.0
Condition of littering	1991	27.8	28.3	24.3	15.3	4.5
	2007	37.0	32.4	20.0	7.7	2.9

Table 19—Summary statistics of all respondents indicating impressions of reserving wilderness permits.

Aspect of permit system	Overnight	Day use
1. How permit was reserved:		
Phone	6.3%	35.3%
Internet	49.2%	54.1%
Mail/Fax	1.0%	10.6%
Someone else in group	30.2%	NA
Did not reserve a permit	3.4%	NA
2. Applied for lottery (before January 15):	(±3.6%)	(±6.2%)
Yes	16.5%	24.2%
No	83.5%	75.8%
If yes, how difficult was this:		
(1 = Difficult, 10 = Easy)	8.12	5.90
	(±.61)	(±1.00)
3. Reserved online via online National Recreation Reservation Service (after January 20):	(±4.8%)	(±9.6%)
Yes	61.8%	43.1%
No	38.2%	56.9%
If yes, how difficult was this:		
(1 = Difficult, 10 = Easy)	8.17	6.29
	(±.28)	(±.96)
4. Received confirmation of reservation?	(±3.0%)	(±8.9%)
Yes	90.1%	80.1%
No	9.9%	18.9%

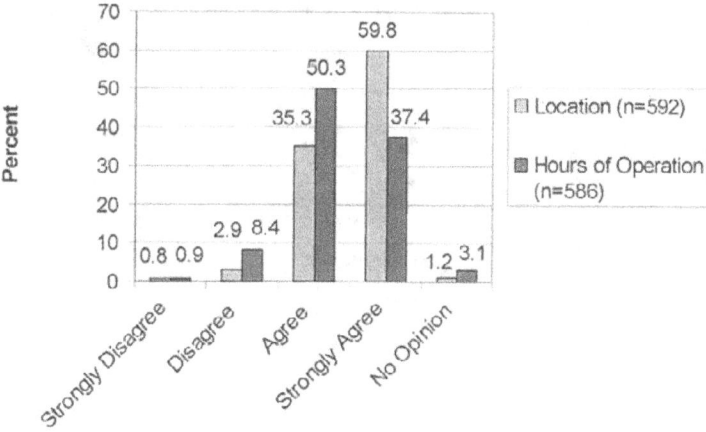

Figure 6—Percentage of agreement with convenience of permit station location and hours.

Table 20—Percentage of overnight visitors indicating impression of fee program.

Aspect of fee program	Strongly disagree	Disagree	Agree	Strongly agree	No opinion
	- percent -				
Use fee deposit ($20) was an appropriate amount	1.8	3.4	62.2	27.9	4.7
Reservation fee ($12) was an appropriate amount	2.0	7.0	63.9	23.0	4.1
Overnight use fee ($10 adult, $5 child/senior) was an appropriate amount	2.2	7.5	61.2	25.2	3.9
Non-Forest Service vendor issuing fee ($2) was an appropriate amount	1.2	3.8	58.4	14.9	21.7
Information about fees was adequate	0.7	3.6	67.9	19.8	8.1
Process of paying fees was easy	0.3	0.9	65.9	28.0	4.9
Boundary Waters is better off due to these fees	1.0	3.8	45.5	38.3	11.5

Figure 7—Over 80% of overnight respondents in 2007 agreed the BWCAW was better off due to fees.

USDA Forest Service Res. Pap. RMRS-RP-91. 2012

Recent Events—In 1999, a massive storm hit northern Minnesota and the BWCAW. Winds in excess of 90 mph caused extensive blowdown on nearly one-half million acres of the BWCAW, downing an estimated 25 million trees (Lime 2000). In 2006 (and subsequently 2007), both management-ignited and lightning-ignited fires burned portions of the BWCAW. Both overnight and day visitors reported if they were aware of these events, and if events affected their plans to visit (Table 21).

Nearly 92% of overnight visitors were aware of the 1999 blowdown storm. However, only 22% of overnight visitors reported that the blowdown area had affected their plans to visit the BWCAW in past years. In terms of their 2007 trip, only 9% of overnight visitors reported the blowdown had affected their plans.

As with the blowdown, the vast majority of overnight visitors (82%) were aware of prescribed burning occurring in the BWCAW. However, only 4% reported it affected their plans in previous years and 2% reported it affected their plans in 2007. Overnight visitors (70%) were also aware of lightning-ignited fires in the BWCAW. Only 8% reported these fires affected their plans in previous years and 11% reported fires affected their plans in 2007.

Day Visitor Respondent Profile in 2007

Another important issue in the BWCAW is the emergence of day use. Previous studies have provided limited insight into this segment of the visitor population. The 2007 study attempted to provide a clearer picture of the day use population. This included both day visitor paddlers (DP) and day visitor motorists (DM).

It is important to note that several challenges presented themselves in contacting and surveying day visitor respondents. When considering sampling locations, opportunities existed to intercept day visitor respondents at Forest Service permit offices, cooperator locations, and onsite at entry points. Regarding Forest Service permit stations, DP visitors very rarely frequented these stations, making DM visitors the primary individuals to sample. However, DM individuals were very few, and appeared mostly to be local residents and repeat visitors. After sampling them once, it made no sense to sample them again.

DM visitors created challenges in data collection for additional reasons as well. DM permits are not self-issue, have a weekly quota, and could be reserved.

Table 21—Percentage of overnight visitors indicating awareness of recent events and effects on planning .

Recent events in the BWCAW	"Yes"
Aware of 1999 storm blowdown:	91.9% (±2.2%)
Blowdown affected plans to visit BWCAW in past years	21.8% (±3.5%)
Blowdown affected plans to visit BWCAW this year	9.2% (±2.3%)
Aware of prescribed burning(management-ignited fires) occurring in BWCAW	82.2% (±3.4%)
Prescribed burning affected plans to visit BWCAW in past years	4.1% (±1.8%)
Prescribed burning affected plans to visit BWCAW this year	2.4% (±1.3%)
Aware of lightning-ignited fires that occurred in BWCAW	69.3% (±3.7%)
Lightning-ignited fires affected plans to visit BWCAW last year (2006)	8.0% (±2.6%)
Lightning-ignited fires affected plans to visit BWCAW this year (2007)	11.1% (±3.0%)

Thus, intercepting the individual when they picked up their permit was not always successful. Second, the role of cooperators in reserving and issuing DM permits created challenges. Some cooperators would reserve multiple day permits as a multi-day trip. Thus, one group could have five permits for 5 days. Visitors may have considered this part of the cooperator's services and thus never considered themselves as part of the reservation/issuing process. In addition, many of these permits are issued at cooperator locations when the visitor arrived, making intercepting those individuals very difficult.

The inability to contact DP visitors was very surprising. Given the number of self-issue permits, the expectation was that these individuals would be frequently intercepted. However, many times there was a complete lack of opportunities to intercept DP visitors. We can only speculate on why DP visitors were so difficult to intercept during the 2007 study. It may have been that individuals were launching from cooperator and private residences and later dropping off the self-issue permits at entry points. It may be that they were launching and returning on very short trips in the 11-3 p.m. window when surveyors were not on site.

The sample of day visitor respondents in 2007 consists of 186 individuals. Given the previous limitations, it is most appropriate to consider the following summarized results as a day visitor respondent profile that warrants

further testing and examination. It is also important to recognize that, while not necessarily representative of the entire population, this profile does provide a unique view of day visitor respondents characteristics, trip characteristics, and visitor attitudes.

Visitor Characteristics—Day visitor respondents answered comparable demographic questions to those asked of overnight visitors (Table 22). The sample provided an average age of 49 years, with approximately 64% of them being male. Respondent's reported median education level consisted of some college experience and only 7% of the sample was currently full-time or part-time students. The median annual income for the day visitor respondents in the sample was $90,000.

The average group size of day visitor respondents in 2007 was 3.6 individuals (Table 23). The maximum party size limit of nine people and four boats that applies to overnight visitors also applies to this sample. Approximately 59% of day visitor respondent groups were composed of family members, with 5% of the sample reporting they were on a solo trip. Of the individuals sampled, none reported being part of an organized group.

Wilderness Experience—Only 8% of day visitor respondents in 2007 were on their first visit to the BWCAW (Table 24). Individuals in the sample reported having, on average, taken over 31 visits to the BWCAW. However, it is important to recognize

Table 22—Sociodemographic characteristics of day visitor respondents.

	Mean age	Med. education	Students %	Females %	Conserv. org %
2007 Day use visitors	49	14	7	36	28

Table 23—Summary statistics of day visitor respondents for visit characteristics.

Visit characteristic	2007 visitors
Solo visitors (%)	4.8
Organized groups (%)	NA
Groups with family members (%)	59.1
Mean group size (people)	3.6

Table 24—Summary statistics of day visitor respondents indicating previous wilderness experience.

Wilderness experience	2007 visitors
First-time to BWCAW (%)	8
Experience in others (%)	78
Previous BWCAW visits	31.4

that each single day visit contributes to this total (e.g. considers a multi-day fishing trip as multiple visits) and the standard deviation for these day visitor respondents is nearly 79 visits. Along with previous experience in the BWCAW, many of these individuals have experience in other wilderness areas. Nearly 80% report having visited other wilderness areas in the past.

Trip Characteristics—Day visitor respondents in 2007 used a variety of methods to travel in the BWCAW (Table 25). Approximately 34% paddled privately owned boats while 21% paddled rented boats. Comparably, 32% used private motorboats on their day trips, while 11% rented motorboats.

Like overnight visitors, fishing was a major activity for day visitor respondents in 2007. Approximately 63% of the sample reported fishing on their day trip, while 53% described fishing as a priority on their day trip (Table 26). In addition, 24% of day visitor respondents reported using a gas stove on their day trip.

Encounter Levels—Day visitor respondents in 2007 reported seeing, on average, 7.5 non-motorized groups and 3.3 motorized groups during the course of their day trip. However, despite these encounter levels, 68% of day visitor respondents in the sample reported that the BWCAW was not overcrowded (Table 27). About one-quarter of the sample felt that the BWCAW was crowded in a few places and only 4% felt it was crowded in most places.

When these encounter levels were compared to visitor expectations, consistently over half of day visitor respondents reported that encounter levels of non-motorized groups, motorized groups, and groups at portages were

Table 25—Percentage of day visitor respondents indicating method of travel.

Method of travel	% of 2007 visitors
Private non-motorized	34
Rented non-motorized	21
Private motorboat	32
Rented motorboat	11

Table 26—Percentage of day visitor respondents indicating trip features.

Trip characteristic	% of 2007 visitors
Fished	63
Fishing a priority	53
Used gas stove	24

Table 27—Percentage of day visitor respondents indicating opinions about crowding.

Visitor opinion	% of 2007 visitors
Not overcrowded	68
Crowded in a few places	24
Crowded in most places	4
Did not notice	4

about what they expected (Table 28). Between 13-15% of those sampled reported that encounters were more or far more than they expected.

Evaluation of Resource Conditions—Similar to overnight visitors, day visitor respondents answered 17 questions about various resource impact issues across the BWCAW (Table 29). For all of these potential issues, at least 80% of respondents in the sample described the issues as not a problem. The largest resource issues for respondents were litter (20.2%), the difficulty of obtaining a day use permit (20.1%), and amount of information on where other users would be (17.3%).

Day visitor respondents also reported about the wear and tear on conditions in the BWCAW and the condition of littering (Table 30). Over 85% of respondents reported they thought wear and tear of conditions were either very good or good. Likewise over 76% of respondents thought the evidence of littering was either very good or good.

Additional Management Issues—As previously described, an additional purpose of this research was to try to understand several things (e.g., wilderness permits, fees, natural disturbances) that had changed since the previous studies that might be facilitating change. Day visitor respondents also answered questions on these additional management issues. The following sections describe the attitudes and evaluations of day visitor respondents for these specific issues.

Wilderness Permits—While DP visitors are required to obtain a free, self-issue permit at entry points, DM permits require a fee and can be reserved in advance. These permits were reserved most frequently online for day visitor respondents (54%) (Table 19). Only 24% of day visitor respondents used the lottery to reserve their permits. For those that did, they found it slightly more easy than difficult. Confirmations of permit reservations were received by 80% of day visitor respondents. Finally, day visitor respondents reported if they had ever reserved an overnight permit for the BWCAW. Nearly half (48.9%) reported that they had previously reserved an overnight permit.

Table 28—Percentage of day visitor respondents indicating expectations for seeing groups.

Type of group encountered	Far fewer	Fewer	About what I expected	More	Far more	Had no expectation
			percent			
Non-motorized groups	3.3	14.1	62.0	10.3	3.3	7.1
Motorized groups	2.2	13.7	57.1	9.9	4.9	12.1
Groups at portages	6.1	10.5	50.3	12.2	2.8	18.2

Table 29—Percentage of day visitor respondents indicating evaluation of conditions.

Problem	Evaluation	
	Not a problem	A problem
	percent	
Portages poorly maintained	92.9	7.1
Litter	79.8	20.2
Inadequate disposal of human body waste	91.3	8.7
Large groups of people	84.7	15.3
Too many people in area	85.5	14.5
Area rule/regulations not adequately publicized	88.6	11.4
Not enough information on where other users like to be	82.7	17.3
Permit requirement not well advertised	83.5	16.5
Process of obtaining day use permit too difficult	79.9	20.1
Not enough parking spaces at wilderness entry points	86.1	13.9
Not enough firewood	88.4	11.6
Improper disposal of fish entrails	90.2	9.8
Low flying aircraft	92.5	7.5
Too many rules/regulations	86.5	13.5
People making noise	87.1	12.9
Fire grates full of charcoal/ash	92.3	7.7
Fire grate full of trash	85.2	14.8

Table 30—Percentage of day visitor respondents indicating evaluation of wear and tear.

Conditions	Very good	Good	Fair	Poor	Very poor
			percent		
Wear and tear of conditions	39.8	45.9	9.9	3.3	0.6
Conditions of littering	41.5	35.1	15.2	3.5	3.5

Recreation Fees—Although only DM permits have applicable fees in terms of day visitor respondents, DP opinions on the fee program were also collected (Table 31). The majority of day visitor respondents supported the various aspects of the fee program. Aspects with the largest amount of disagreement were the amount of the reservation fee (16%) and the amount of overnight use fees (17%), the vendor issuing fee (11%), and the use fee deposit (10%). However, 87% of day visitor respondents agreed that they were better off due to these fees and 88% agreed that the BWCAW was better off due to these fees.

Recent Events—The vast majority of day visitor respondents (85%) in 2007 were aware of the 1999 blowdown storm (Table 32). However, only 18% of day visitor respondents reported that the blowdown area had affected their plans to visit the BWCAW in past years. In terms of their 2007 trip, only 5% of day visitor respondents reported the blowdown had affected their plans.

Table 31—Percentage of day visitor respondents indicating impression of fee program.

Aspect of fee program	Strongly disagree	Disagree	Agree	Strongly agree	No opinion
	- percent -				
Use fee deposit ($20) was an appropriate amount	2.8	6.8	67.2	14.1	9.0
Reservation fee ($12) was an appropriate amount	5.6	10.6	64.8	10.6	8.4
Overnight use fee ($10 adult, $5 child/senior) was an appropriate amount	6.2	11.3	66.1	9.0	7.3
Non-Forest Service vendor issuing fee ($2) was an appropriate amount	3.4	7.9	68.0	6.7	14.0
Information about fees was adequate	1.7	6.2	72.9	5.6	13.6
Process of paying fees was easy	0.6	2.3	74.0	9.6	13.6
You are better off due to these fees	5.1	7.9	55.6	11.8	19.7
Boundary Waters is better off due to these fees	5.0	6.7	57.5	17.9	12.8

Table 32—Percentage of day visitor respondents indicating awareness of recent events and effects on planning.

Recent events in the BWCAW	"Yes"
Aware of 1999 storm blowdown:	84.9% (±5.2%)
Blowdown affected plans to visit BWCAW in past years	17.9% (±5.9%)
Blowdown affected plans to visit BWCAW this year	4.9% (±3.3%)
Aware of prescribed burning (management-ignited fires) occurring in BWCAW	76.1% (±6.2%)
Prescribed burning affected plans to visit BWCAW in past years	1.4% (±2.0%)
Prescribed burning affected plans to visit BWCAW this year	2.1% (±2.4%)
Aware of lightning-ignited fires that occurred in BWCAW	72.3% (±6.5%)
Lightning-ignited fires affected plans to visit BWCAW last year (2006)	6.7% (±4.2%)
Lightning-ignited fires affected plans to visit BWCAW this year (2007)	10.4% (±5.1%)

As with the blowdown, a clear majority of day visitor respondents (76%) were aware of prescribed burning occurring in the BWCAW (Table 32). However, less than 4% reported it affected their plans in previous years and less than 2% reported it affected their plans in 2007. Respondents were also aware of lightning-ignited fires in the BWCAW (72%). Less than 8% reported these fires affected their plans in previous years and less than 11% reported fires affected their plans in 2007.

Discussion

The purpose of this research has been to determine trends in overnight use and user characteristics at the BWCAW and to inform managers about current visitors. Trends revealed several interesting outcomes, including constancy in gender proportions over time, some notable changes in demographics of visitors, changes in conservation organization membership, the importance of fishing as an activity, and response to encounter levels. The following sections further explore several of these concepts.

Gender Ratio Stability

As observed in Table 5, the male to female gender ratio has remained relatively stable over time. That is, 70-75% of BWCAW overnight visitors have been male over the past 40 years. While day use proportions of females were higher, it has previously been suggested that generally in the United States the proportion of females engaging in wilderness activities was increasing (Watson 2000). That trend comes into question with these BWCAW results and those by Bowker and others (2006). It would also be naïve to assume that this trend has emerged at the BWCAW because wilderness paddling and/or boating is a recreation opportunity inherently favored by men. Thus, the stability of the gender ratio in the BWCAW may be potentially understood if female constraints and barriers to participation and inclusion are considered.

Previous research has examined how gender creates barriers to leisure participation (see Jackson and Henderson 1995, Little 2002). Particularly, socio-cultural stereotypes have depicted adventure and wilderness experiences as simulating "voyageur" travels and opportunities for male bonding. These stereotypes depict some outdoor leisure pursuits as not appropriate for women or their gender role due to their lack of strength, skill, and experience. Unfortunately, such stereotypes have also created perceptions in some women that they are not competent or lack the technical skills for wilderness activities and experiences (McDermott 2004).

Women further may lack confidence and self-esteem to attempt these pursuits, be influenced by peer pressure, or lack female role models in the activity (Culp 1998). Regrettably, the perpetuation and reinforcements of these inappropriate stereotypes and perceptions represent significant barriers for women to participate in outdoor and adventures experiences.

McDermott (2004) and Little (2002) have explored ways for women to negotiate and overcome these constraints, but they still exist and women still individually need to overcome them. Therefore, if these stereotypes and constraints exist or are being proliferated in the BWCAW context, that may be a possible explanation for the disproportionate use of the BWCAW by female participants. Potential female participants, (and male participants as well for that matter) may see the BWCAW as a place that is too challenging or that wilderness paddling and travel as a recreation activity requires technical skills they have yet to learn. Potential female participants may also feel peer pressure from both male and female companions to avoid these types of experiences and therefore chose to recreate elsewhere and in other ways.

A second potential explanation for the stability of gender ratios are individual experience levels. Trends in BWCAW experience levels demonstrated that many respondents are repeat visitors. If women are not repeatedly taking trips, encouraged to participate, or included in trips with others, it may become difficult for them to consider paddling in the BWCAW as a recreation opportunity in the future. A barrier for women to become repeat visitors could be created. Likewise, finding groups of female friends with similar motivations and expectations could be a challenge. While all-female groups are encountered during trips into the BWCAW, results suggest this is not the norm. Women may be able to find other women who enjoy hiking, camping, or other outdoor activities, but for various reasons it may be difficult to develop that cohort of friends wanting to engage in a paddling setting. Finally, other consideration and exploration is necessary if the phenomena of gender ratio differences are to be studied further. It is yet to be determined whether this is something unique to the BWCAW contextually, or follows predictions and trends in female wilderness participation elsewhere.

Demographic Trends

The demographic profile of BWCAW overnight visitors could best be described as getting older, having more education, less being full or part-time students (Table 5) and enduringly white. By examining these trends first in

1969, it can be seen that mean age of overnight visitors was 26, most had a high school education, and nearly half were currently students. By 2007, that mean age had risen to 45, with most having a college degree, and only about 10% being students.

This trend may be explained if respondents are considered as a stable cohort of visitors. That is, while the individual studies were not panel studies that sampled the same respondents, the same defined population was sampled. With the high proportion of repeat visitors and high frequency of visits, it is possible that the trends studies have been following this same visitor cohort over the past 40 years, from the time nearly half were under 26 to the present when over half are over 45. They were first intercepted when they were young adults and still in school. Then they were contacted in the early 90s, having completed college and continuing to visit the BWCAW. Lastly, they were contacted in 2007 as they approach or pass middle age. While it is important to recognize that younger individuals and first time overnight visitors continue to use the BWCAW, trend data suggest that a strong and substantial cohort of aging, repeat visitors to the BWCAW exists.

In the case of day use, these visitors appear to be older with a mean age of 49, even less are full or part-time students (7%), and with a larger proportion of females (Table 22). These visitors also average more trips than overnight users with over 30 previous visits to the BWCAW. However, this number varies greatly. These demographic differences, compared to overnight visitors could be at least partly due to safety concerns. As visitors age, issues of ability and physical limitations may arise. It could be safer to take a day trip versus an extended overnight trip in the BWCAW. Demographic differences may also be due to convenience. It may be more convenient for older visitors to take numerous day trips compared to younger visitors who may only be able to plan a single extended overnight trip to the BWCAW due to time constraints.

Organization Membership

Examination of membership in an outdoor recreation or conservation organization also showed a dramatic shift from 1969 to 2007. In 1969, only 12% of overnight visitors reported being a member in an outdoor recreation or conservation organization. This proportion increased significantly to 35% in 1991 and then decreased to 29% in 2007. These changes may be associated with an increase in the number and size of conservation and environmental organizations from 1970

to 1990 (see Mitchell and others 1992). However, these results are also similar to trends in visitors of Oregon's Eagle Cap Wilderness. Watson and others (1996) compared visitors from 1965 and 1993 to examine trends in wilderness attitudes. Similar to results in the BWCAW, Watson and others found that the number of visitors who belonged to outdoor recreation or conservation organizations increased from 25% in 1965 to 44% in 1993. They suggest this as a factor influencing the strength of wilderness values and reflect a more sophisticated visitor population (higher than normal education, friends that visit wilderness, membership in conservation organizations). A similar argument can be made in the BWCAW. Overall education of overnight visitors has increased and membership in outdoor recreation and conservation organizations has increased. This may indicate a visitor population in which the strength of wilderness attitudes and values has increased over time. Such an argument is important to managers because it suggests an invested constituency exists for the BWCAW. Thus, understanding any shifts and changes in this constituency's attitudes and values should remain a priority to BWCAW managers.

Shifts in Fishing

An interesting shift from 1991 to 2007 was the percentage of overnight visitors reporting they fished during their trip and that fishing was a priority on their trip (Figure 8). This trend is also consistent with national trends in fishing and hunting. Data from the 2006 National

Figure 8—Of respondents who fished, 47% described fishing as a major reason for their trip in 1991 compared to 35% in 2007.

Survey of Fishing, Hunting, and Wildlife-Associated Recreation suggest that the percentage of individuals nationally who participated in fishing has decreased from 21% in 1991 to 13.1% in 2006 (USFWS 2006).

Several explanations are possible for this shift. One possible explanation is a shift in activity specialization and mode of travel for overnight BWCAW visitors. In 1991, 72% of visitors traveled in private non-motorized boats and 18% in rented non-motorized boats. This significantly changed by 2007 to 68% in private boats and 26% in rented boats. Private motorboats saw a significant decrease by 2007 (Table 13). Thus, it may be that visitors less specialized in wilderness paddling or boating as an activity, may also be less interested in fishing. The nature of the activity of wilderness paddling and boating may be changing such that fishing has slowly become less of an essential component of the experience.

Another explanation of a shift in fishing could be associated to a regional shift in the definition of a BWCAW experience. In both 1991 and 2007, over 60% of overnight visitors were Minnesota residents. Over this period, the place of residence for respondents changed to represent less agricultural communities and more metropolitan centers and urbanization (Table 12). While no BWCAW overnight visitors grew up in a metropolitan area in 1991, over 16% did in 2007. Only 4% of visitors currently live on agricultural farms, whereas over 44% now live in cities of 50,000 people or more. This shift towards urbanization reflects a population where children are exposed less and less to fishing, camping, and canoeing. Activities such as these may not be emphasized as much in current generations as in previous ones. Therefore, shifts toward urbanization may relate to a decrease in fishing as an activity essential to a wilderness experience in the BWCAW.

A link with experience levels in wilderness could be a potential factor in the decrease in fishing as well; 94% of overnight visitors are repeat visitors and 75% have experience in other wilderness areas. Additionally, many of these individuals began visiting wilderness areas by their early 20's (Table 7). While a high level of wilderness experience is represented in the BWCAW, a link to younger cohort groups may exist. While this represents a strong cohort of individuals 45 and older across this trend study, a smaller cohort group of individuals under 25 also exists. This cohort of emerging adults may represent those individuals who have not grown up fishing and thus participate less in fishing and do not place as great a priority on fishing as other cohort groups in the study.

Resource Condition Evaluation

When asked to evaluate 19 resource issues, nine appeared to improve significantly from 1991 to 2007 (Table 17). Perceptions of wear and tear of conditions in the BWCAW also appear to have improved. However, some inconsistencies are present, such as litter evaluated as improving but still ranked as the top resource issue for the BWCAW. While many of these improvements can be attributed to direct management actions, policy changes, and better information and education, factors such as experience levels and urbanization, may be linked to the inconsistencies in visitor evaluations. Visitors with high levels of experience have a greater basis for comparison than first time or infrequent visitors. They have seen the changes across the BWCAW and may perceive that these problems are not as big as once believed. They may consider conditions adequate given the high level of use in the BWCAW or compared to the other wilderness areas they have visited.

A trend of increased urbanization in Minnesota as suggested by respondent's place of residence may also be a factor in decreased perceptions of problems. Compared to metropolitan and urban areas, the natural areas of the BWCAW are pristine in terms of litter, wear and tear, and resource damage. They are a stark contrast to the noise, crowding, and maintenance of the city. Individuals who have grown up in these urban areas may have a different perception of wilderness conditions and therefore do not recognize or strongly criticize resource conditions as individuals who have grown up in more rural settings. Thus, despite giving credit to BWCAW managers for improvements in resource condition, it is important to consider that other factors correlate to visitor's perceived improvements in resource conditions.

Inter-Group Encounters and Expectations

Encountering large groups of people was the one management issue that increased as a problem from 1991 to 2007 (Figure 9). Visitors also reported significantly higher inter-group encounters over the duration of their trip, from about 4 encounters per day in 1991 to over 8 in 2007 (Table 10). However, an increased number of visitors reporting that their expectation for seeing groups was exceeded did not occur. Instead, over half of overnight visitors in 2007 reported that inter-group encounters were about what they expected. These results are consistent with results from other wilderness areas (see Cole and Hall 2008). This may suggest that while an erosion of the quality of the wilderness experience may

Figure 9—Launch points are areas where a high number of inter-group encounters may occur.

be occurring in terms of encounters, there is evidence of increased acceptance of inter-group encounters and social conditions by visitors. Thus, the reports of seeing more groups, a lack of privacy, and increased congestion may not be significantly challenging an individual's expectations when it comes to inter-group encounters.

Understanding the nature of these expectations will be important for BWCAW managers in the future. Due to higher past experience levels, were visitors better informed? Are they simply prepared to see more people? Visitors also now have more access to information regarding travel patterns, congestion, and crowding at the BWCAW. Travel websites, outfitters, and the media can all provide them with information to help them make travel plans. Maps also provide information about which lakes have a greater number of campsites. Are managers preparing them more for congestion in certain areas (e.g. portages, entry points) and for the issues that arise related to the change in social conditions? Managers make efforts to inform visitors which areas are more heavily used due to having a higher quota of permits. Suggestions can be made about which times and days of the week will be less congested. All of these factors might be contributing to overnight visitors having expectations for having a higher number of inter-group encounters than in the past.

Repeat visitors have seen changes in visitation over time and may have incrementally adjusted their expectations for inter-group encounters. When selecting to travel through high use entry points and congested areas, they are prepared for frequent encounters and large groups. Their trips may focus more on enjoying scenic beauty and exploring than seeking out privacy opportunities. On the other hand, is it as simple as those visitors who increasingly live in urban areas having a higher expectation and acceptance of encounters? That is, the amount of congestion in the BWCAW is less compared to that of their increasingly congested everyday lives.

All of these factors will need consideration as managers continue to address crowding and congestion issues across the BWCAW. It suggests that things that are more important may matter to visitors than simply the number of people they encounter. One of these things that may be critical is a sense of freedom and perceived control. Despite a desire for privacy and solitude, they may value freedom to travel where they want, when they want, and to explore even more (see also Cole and Hall 2008). Quite simply, they might be resolved to not let other visitors impede or impose upon their experience. Such behaviors and expectations could have important management implications. It suggests that managers may need a more precise understanding of how visitor travel patterns, motivations for camping, and the quota system influences the social conditions across the BWCAW.

Sampling Day Visitor Respondents

While the 2007 sampling strategy had some opportunities to contact day visitor respondents, it appears that different strategies are necessary to improve the number of contacts. Specifically, individual sampling strategies are probably necessary for DM and DP visitors. Such strategies would probably require additional assistance from local cooperators. In future research, efficiently and effectively contacting day visitor respondents will remain a challenge. In addition, it will be necessary to determine if they cross wilderness boundaries and effectively how far they travel into wilderness zones. In some instances, such as Hegman Lake and many of the motor routes, these travel patterns may be very consistent given geographical limitations. For others, they may vary considerably. Further thought and discussion with Superior National Forest staff is also necessary to better understand the issues and trends related to day visitor respondents.

Conclusions

Examining trends in wilderness areas can help us to determine the future direction and implications of our management policies and actions. This trends study in the BWCAW has shown how use and user characteristics have been changing over the last 40 years. It reveals that BWCAW overnight visitors are predominantly white, male, well educated, and no longer full or part time students. Visitors have a great deal of wilderness trip experience in the BWCAW and in other wilderness areas as well, with relatively few visitors being first time visitors to the area. Visitors also report seeing significantly more groups while on their trip compared to previous years and visits. However, these inter-group encounter rates are well within the expectations visitors have for the area. Whether through information, education, or better preparation, visitors seem to have a good idea of how many groups they will encounter while in the BWCAW.

Visitors have also evaluated how resource conditions have been changing in the BWCAW. Seeing large groups is an increasing problem, but many issues have improved: portage maintenance, fish entrails disposal, and litter. It is also important to recognize that researchers, managers, and visitors perceive issues such as congestion at portages and destruction of vegetation differently.

Researchers and managers perceive portage congestion and destruction of vegetation as bigger problems than what is perceived and reported by visitors. While issues of importance may change, this trend study has provided a new baseline for resource impact evaluation by visitors. It has also provided new baselines for visitor attitudes toward fees, use permits, and the variety of natural disturbances and forces operating across the BWCAW landscape. These baselines will be useful for managers in determining how to prioritize management issues and for understanding how visitors will perceive management actions directed at these issues.

This trend study also provides a preliminary profile for day visitor respondents in the BWCAW, something previously not attempted in depth. It suggests that day visitor respondents are highly experienced and frequently visiting the BWCAW. Similar to overnight visitors, they are seeing many groups, but not exceeding expectations. They also are supportive of permits, fees, and are aware of the various natural disturbances that have occurred across the BWCAW recently and in the past. While this profile might not be generalizable to all day visitor respondents to the BWCAW, it is the first step in understanding a population that is a significant portion of wilderness users in the BWCAW. It also demonstrates the influence they potentially have on overnight and other visitors within the BWCAW. Thus, understanding their travel behaviors and attitudes relative to other visitors will be critical to gain an understanding of how different visitor types influence each other's experiences.

In addition to profiling trends and changes in use and users, this study also starts to address questions about future wilderness users. Potts (2007) has recently challenged managers and researchers to consider the implications of changing human relationships with wilderness. He argues that the meaning of wilderness for today's user is not necessarily that of the individuals championing wilderness in the 1960s and 1970s. All users are a product of their experiences and conditions that surround their interactions with wilderness.

For example, the BWCAW user cohort has many experiences from which to create their perception of wilderness areas. They have seen changes in social and resource conditions over the course of their visits. They can compare these changes to experiences that they have had in other areas. However, what of the emerging adults under 25 and those who are first time visitors to wilderness? What do they base their perceptions on and in turn, how will this affect their meanings and value for wilderness? Potts (2007) cautions that as relationships change, there is also a potential for the wilderness constituency to change or even disappear. He questions what will happen if apathy and irrelevance toward wilderness begins to prevail in the public's eyes.

For these reasons, it is important to continue to examine and determine the changes in wilderness use and user characteristics. Researchers and managers can continue to benefit from understanding how perceptions of visitors change in relationship to changing resource and social conditions. With strong baselines and knowledge of changing trends, managers can create sound policy and plan for changing conditions. They can outline management actions that will provide opportunities for future individuals to having meaningful wilderness experiences while protecting wilderness character and relationships.

References

Borrie, W. T., and McCool, S. F. (2007). Describing change in visitors and visits to the "Bob." International Journal of Wilderness, 13(3), 28-33.

Bowker, J. M., Murphy, D., Cordell, H. K., English, D. B. K., Bergstrom, J. C., Starbuck, C. M., Betz, C. J., and Green, G. T. (2006). Wilderness and primate area recreation participation and consumption: an examination of demographic and spatial factors. Journal of Agricultural and Applied Economic, 38(2), 317-326.

Cole, D. N., and Hall, T. E. (2008). Wilderness visitors, experiences, and management preferences: How they vary with use level and length of stay (Res. Pap. RMRS-RP-71): USDA Forest Service, Rocky Mountain Research Station.

Cole, D. N., Watson, A. E., and Roggenbuck, J. W. (1995). Trends in wilderness visitors and visits: Boundary Waters Canoe Area, Shining Rock, and Desolation Wildernesses (No. INT-RP-483). Ogden, UT: USDA Forest Service, Intermountain Research Station.

Culp, R. H. (1998). Adolescent girls and outdoor recreation: a case study examining constraints and effective programming. Journal of Leisure Research, 30(3), 356-379.

Dillman, D. A. (2007). Mail and internet surveys: the Tailored Design Method (2nd ed.). Hoboken, New Jersey: John Wiley.

Jackson, E. L., and Henderson, K.A. (1995). Gender-based analysis of leisure constraints. Leisure Sciences, 17(1), 31-51.

Lime, D. W. (2000). Human response to large-scale natural disturbances: wilderness visitors' perceptions of 1999 storm-damaged vegetation in Minnesota's Boundary Waters Canoe Area Wilderness. St. Paul, MN: University of Minnesota, Department of Forest Resources.

Little, D. E. (2002). Women and adventure education: reconstructing leisure constraints and adventure experiences to negotiate continuing participation. Journal of Leisure Research, 34(2), 157-177.

Lucas, R. C. (1985). Visitor characteristics, attitudes, and use patterns in the Bob Marshall Wilderness complex, 1970-82. (Res. Pap. INT-345), USDA Forest Service, Intermountain Forest and Range Experiment Station.

Merriam, L. C., and Smith, C. K. (1974). Visitor impact on newly developed campsites in the Boundary Waters Canoe Area. Journal of Forestry, 627-630.

McDermott, L. (2004). Exploring intersections of physicality and female-only canoeing experiences. Leisure Studies, 23(3), 283-301.

Mitchell, R. C., Mertig, A. G., and Dunlap, R. E. (1992). Twenty years of environmental mobilization. In R. E. Dunlap and A. G. Mertig (Eds), American environmentalism: The U.S. environmental movement, 1970–1990 (pp. 11-26). Philadelphia: Taylor and Francis.

Potts, R. (2007). Changing human relationships with wilderness and wildlands: implications for managers. International Journal of Wilderness, 13(3), 4-8, 11.

Stankey, G. H. (1971). The perception of wilderness recreation carrying capacity: a geographic study in natural resources management. Unpublished dissertation, Michigan State University, East Lansing, MI.

Stankey, G. H. (1973). Visitor perceptions of wilderness recreation carrying capacity. (No. INT-142). Odgen, UT: U.S. Department of Agriculture, Forest Service, Intermountain Forest and Range Experiment Station.

U.S. Fish and Wildlife Service. (2006). Trends in fishing and hunting 1991-2006: a focus on fishing and hunting by specie. Addendum to the 2006 national survey of fishing, hunting, and wildlife-associated recreation. Report 2006-8. U.S. Department of the Interior (USDI), Fish and Wildlife Service.

U.S. Forest Service. (2004). Land and Resource Management Plan: Superior National Forest. Milwaukee, WI: Eastern Region, U.S. Department of Agriculture (USDA), Forest Service.

U.S. Forest Service. (2011). Land Areas of the National Forest System. (No. FS-383). Washington, D.C.: U.S. Department of Agriculture (USDA), Forest Service.

Watson, A. E. (1995). Opportunities for solitude in the Boundary Waters Canoe Area Wilderness. Northern Journal of Applied Forestry, 12(1), 12-18.

Watson, A. E. (2000). Wilderness use in the year 2000: societal changes that influence human relationships with wilderness. In: Cole, David N.; McCool, Stephen F.; Borrie, William T.; O'Loughlin, Jennifer, comps. 2000. Wilderness science in a time of change conference-Volume 4: Wilderness visitors, experiences, and visitor management; 1999 May 23 27; Missoula, MT. Proceedings RMRS-P-15-VOL-4. Ogden, UT: U.S. Department of Agriculture, Forest Service, Rocky Mountain Research Station: 53–60.

Watson, A. E., and Cronn, R. (1994). How previous experience relates to visitors' perceptions of wilderness conditions. Trends, 31(3), 43-46.

Watson, A. E., Hendee, J. C., and Zaglauer, H. P. (1996). Human values and codes of behavior: Changes in Oregon's Eagle Cap Wilderness visitors and their attitudes. Natural Areas Journal, 16(2), 89-93.

Appendix

Boundary Waters Canoe Area Wilderness

Visitor Study

2007 Summer Season
Overnight Visits

Aldo Leopold Wilderness Research Institute
790 E. Beckwith Ave.
Missoula, MT 59801

This survey is voluntary. While you are not required to respond, your cooperation is needed to make the survey results comprehensive, accurate, and timely. You may be assured that in the analysis and reporting of the results, your answers will not be connected with you.

YOUR OVERNIGHT VISIT TO THE BOUNDARY WATERS CANOE AREA WILDERNESS
THAT BEGAN ON: _____/_____, 2007

---

1. How did you travel in the wilderness on this visit? (Check all that apply, but if more than one, underline the way you traveled <u>most</u>.)

☐ PADDLED A PRIVATELY OWNED WATER CRAFT
☐ PADDLED A WATER CRAFT RENTED FROM A COMMERCIAL OUTFITTER
☐ MOTORED IN A PRIVATELY OWNED WATER CRAFT
☐ MOTORED IN A WATER CRAFT RENTED FROM A COMMERCIAL OUTFITTER
☐ OTHER (Describe) _____

2a. Did you fish on this trip? (Circle one response)   1. Yes   2. No

2b. Was fishing a major reason for going on this trip? (Circle one response)
                                                             1. Yes   2. No

3. During <u>this overnight visit</u> to the Boundary Waters:

    a. Did you use a gas stove for cooking? (Circle one response)
                                                             1. Yes   2. No

    b. How many times on your trip did
   you have a wood fire?   _____TIMES

   How many of these wood fires
   were in the evening?   _____FIRES

   How many of these evening fires
   were to sit around and
   enjoy - - <u>not for cooking</u>?   _____FIRES

    c. Was the number of campfires you had influenced by fire restrictions? (Circle one response)   1. Yes   2. No

4. Please <u>estimate</u> the following for your wilderness visit: (Enter a number in all three columns for each item)

	Least in a Single Day	Most in a Single Day	Total For Trip
a. the number of nonmotorized groups you saw	_____	_____	_____
b. the number of motorized groups you saw	_____	_____	_____
c. the number of groups that camped within sight or sound of your campsite	_____	_____	_____
d. the number of groups that paddled or motored within sight or sound of your campsite	_____	_____	_____

5. How did the following compare with what you <u>expected</u> to see in the Boundary Waters? (Circle one scale response for each statement)

	Far Fewer	Fewer	About What I Expected	More	Far More	Had no Expectation
a. the number of nonmotorized groups you saw	FF	F	E	M	FM	X
b. the number of motorized groups you saw	FF	F	E	M	FM	X
c. the number of groups that camped within sight or sound of your campsite	FF	F	E	M	FM	X
d. the number of groups that paddled/motored within sight or sound of your campsite	FF	F	E	M	FM	X
e. the number of groups you saw at portages	FF	F	E	M	FM	X

USDA Forest Service Res. Pap. RMRS-RP-91. 2012

6.How did the following compare with what you preferred to see in the Boundary Waters? (Circle one scale response for each statement)

	Far Fewer	Fewer	About What I Preferred	More	Far More	Had no Preference
a. the number of nonmotorized groups you saw	FF	F	P	M	FM	X
b. the number of motorized groups you saw	FF	F	P	M	FM	X
c. the number of groups that camped within sight or sound of your campsite	FF	F	P	M	FM	X
d. the number of groups that paddled/motored within sight or sound of your campsite	FF	F	P	M	FM	X
e. the number of groups you saw at portages	FF	F	P	M	FM	X

7. This set of items concerns problems you may have run into on your visits to the Boundary Waters. Please indicate two things for each item. First, tell us whether you felt the item was a problem during the visit. Second, whether you currently feel the item is a problem or not, indicate whether you feel the situation has become better or worse over the years you have been coming to the Boundary Waters. If this was your first trip, or if you really don't know the trend, indicate by circling the X for 'Don't Know.'

	First, is it:		Second, is it:		
	Not a Problem	A Problem	Getting Better	Getting Worse	Don't Know
a. Portages poorly maintained	N	Y	+	−	X
b. Opportunities to see wildlife	N	Y	+	−	X
c. Destruction of vegetation at or around campsites	N	Y	+	−	X
d. Finding a campsite	N	Y	+	−	X
e. Not enough privacy in campsites	N	Y	+	−	X
f. Litter	N	Y	+	−	X
g. Inadequate disposal of human body waste	N	Y	+	−	X
h. Large groups of people	N	Y	+	−	X
i. Too many people in area you visited	N	Y	+	−	X
j. Congestion at portages	N	Y	+	−	X
k. Area rules and regulations not adequately publicized	N	Y	+	−	X
l. Not enough information on where other users are likely to be	N	Y	+	−	X
m. The wilderness permit requirement is not well advertised	N	Y	+	−	X
n. The process of obtaining available permits is too difficult	N	Y	+	−	X
o. Not enough parking spaces at wilderness entry points	N	Y	+	−	X
p. Not enough firewood	N	Y	+	−	X
q. Campfire restrictions	N	Y	+	−	X
r. Areas closed due to fire	N	Y	+	−	X

USDA Forest Service Res. Pap. RMRS-RP-91. 2012

7. Continued…

		First, is it:		Second, is it:		
		Not a Problem	A Problem	Getting Better	Getting Worse	Don't Know
s.	Fire hazard from downed trees	N	Y	+	–	X
t.	Too many day users	N	Y	+	–	X
u.	Improper disposal of fish entrails	N	Y	+	–	X
v.	Low flying aircraft	N	Y	+	–	X
w.	Too many rules and regulations	N	Y	+	–	X
x.	People making noise	N	Y	+	–	X
y.	Natural condition of fish habitat	N	Y	+	–	X
z.	Fire grates full of charcoal and ashes	N	Y	+	–	X
aa.	Fire grates full of trash	N	Y	+	–	X
ab.	Nuisance bears	N	Y	+	–	X
ac.	Smoke from wildland fires	N	Y	+	–	X
ad.	Aircraft activity for fire management	N	Y	+	–	X
ae.	Amount of burned area	N	Y	+	–	X
af.	Finding an unoccupied campsite	N	Y	+	–	X

If it was a problem, why:

_____

ag.	Presence of inappropriate technology	N	Y	+	–	X

If presence of technology was a problem, please list examples:

_____

_____

8. Did you feel that the Boundary Waters was too crowded? (Circle one)

    1. NO, IT DIDN'T APPEAR OVERCROWDED TO ME
    2. YES, BUT ONLY IN A FEW AREAS
    3. YES, IT WAS OVERCROWDED IN MOST PLACES
    4. I DIDN'T NOTICE ONE WAY OR THE OTHER

9. If you felt that the Boundary Waters was overcrowded, did it bother you? (Circle one)

    1. NO, NOT AT ALL
    2. ONLY A LITTLE
    3. A MODERATE AMOUNT
    4. IT BOTHERED ME A LOT
    5. NOT APPLICABLE

10. If you felt that the Boundary Waters was crowded, did you in any way change the route of your trip or the length of your stay? (Circle one)

    1. NO
    2. LENGTH OF TRIP
    3. ROUTE OF TRIP
    4. BOTH
    5. NOT APPLICABLE

11. If you felt that the Boundary Waters was crowded, will it affect your future plans for visiting? (Circle one)

    1. YES
    2. NO
    3. NOT APPLICABLE

12. How did you feel about the condition of the Boundary Waters in terms of wear and tear from use (erosion and loss of vegetation) and in terms of littering? (Circle one response in each column)

	WEAR AND TEAR	LITTERING	
VERY GOOD	VG	VG	
GOOD	G	G	If you felt there were poor
FAIR	F	F	conditions, where did you
POOR	P	P	observe these? _____
VERY POOR	VP	VP	_____
DO NOT REMEMBER	X	X	_____
			_____

USDA Forest Service Res. Pap. RMRS-RP-91. 2012

13. Different people desire different things from wilderness and managers need to know what things you find acceptable and what things you find unacceptable.

For each characteristic below, we ask that you make three types of judgments

i. Is there a range of values along the scale provided that is **completely unacceptable**? If so, please indicate the unacceptable range by drawing a line above it.

ii. Is there a range of values that would be **acceptable**? If so, please indicate with a line below the scale.

iii. Is there a point on this scale that is most **preferred**? If so, please indicate by placing an x on that point.

PLEASE REMEMBER: NOT DRAWING A LINE OR PLACING AN X IS OKAY, BUT THIS MEANS YOU ARE EITHER UNCERTAIN OR DON'T CARE ABOUT THAT ITEM.

Example: The percent of time other canoeists or boaters are in sight during my visit.

UNACCEPTABLE

| ---- | ---- | ---- X ---- | ---- | ---- ⌐---- | ---- | ---- | ---- |
0   10   20   30   40   50   60   70   80   90   100

_____
ACCEPTABLE

This person **prefers** other visitors in sight about 30% of the time, but 0 – 40% is **acceptable**; more than 60% of the time is **unacceptable**; this person is uncertain about the acceptability of values between 40 and 60%.

---

a. The number of nonmotorized groups I see each day while traveling in the area.

| ---- | ---- | ---- | ---- | ---- | ---- | ---- | ---- | ---- | ---- |
0   10   20   30   40   50

b. The number of motorized groups I see each day while traveling in the area.

| ---- | ---- | ---- | ---- | ---- | ---- | ---- | ---- | ---- |
0   10   20   30   40   50

c. The number of groups camped within sight or sound of my campsite each night.

| ---- | ---- | ---- | ---- | ---- | ---- | ---- | ---- | ---- | ---- |
0   10   20   30   40   50

d. The number of groups who paddle or motor within sight or sound of my campsite each day.

| ---- | ---- | ---- | ---- | ---- | ---- | ---- | ---- | ---- | ---- |
0   10   20   30   40   50

e.   The number of groups I see at a given portage.

| ---- | ---- | ---- | ---- | ---- | ---- | ---- | ---- | ---- | ---- |
0   4   8   12   16   20

14. Please tell us how you feel about the following aspects of the permit system at the Boundary Waters.

RESERVING A PERMIT:

a. How did you reserve your permit: (Circle one response)

    1.   Phone
    2.   Internet
    3.   Mail / FAX
    4.   I didn't reserve a permit, someone else in my group did [Skip to Q. 14e.]
    5.   Our group didn't reserve a permit [Skip to Q. 14e.]

b. Did you apply to the lottery (before January 15) to reserve your permit? (Circle one response)

    1.   No
    2.   Yes

If Yes, how difficult was this: (Mark an X on the scale)

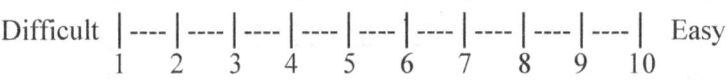

Difficult | ---- | ---- | ---- | ---- | ---- | ---- | ---- | ---- | ---- | Easy
          1   2   3   4   5   6   7   8   9   10

Suggestions for improving the lottery?

_____
_____

c. Did you reserve your permit (after January 20) via the online National Recreation Reservation Service (e.g Recreation.gov)? (Circle one response)

    1.   No
    2.   Yes

If Yes, how difficult was this: (Mark an X on the scale)

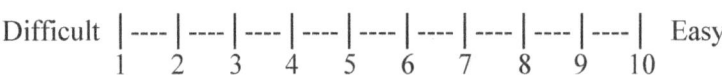

Difficult | ---- | ---- | ---- | ---- | ---- | ---- | ---- | ---- | ---- | Easy
          1   2   3   4   5   6   7   8   9   10

Suggestions for improving the online service?

_____
_____

USDA Forest Service Res. Pap. RMRS-RP-91. 2012

d. Did you receive a confirmation of your reservation? (Circle one response)

    1. No
    2. Yes

Suggestions for improving the confirmation?

_____

_____

PICKING UP YOUR PERMIT:

e. Did you pick up your permit at: (Circle on response)

    1. Forest Service Station
    2. Cooperator Permit Station
        (eg. Lodge or outfitter)

	Strongly Disagree	Disagree	Agree	Strongly Agree	No Opinion
f. The location you picked up your permit was convenient. (Circle one response)	SD	D	A	SA	NO

If you disagree, do you have suggestions for improving the location?

_____

_____

	Strongly Disagree	Disagree	Agree	Strongly Agree	No Opinion
g. The hours of operation at the permit station were convenient. (Circle one response)	SD	D	A	SA	NO

If you disagree, do you have suggestions for improving the hours of operation?

_____

_____

15. Please tell us how you feel about these aspects of the fee program at the Boundary Waters: (Circle one scale response each for questions a through g)

	Strongly Disagree	Disagree	Agree	Strongly Agree	No Opinion
a. The use fee deposit (refundable up to two days before the trip) ($20) was an appropriate amount.	SD	D	A	SA	NO

If you disagree, what do you suggest? _____

b. The reservation fee
(nonrefundable) ($12) was
an appropriate amount.   SD   D   A   SA   NO

If you disagree, what do you suggest? _____

c. The overnight use fee
(per person per trip) ($10
adult, $5 child/senior) was
an appropriate amount.   SD   D   A   SA   NO

If you disagree, what do you suggest? _____

d. The issuing fee (paid to
non-Forest Service vendors)
of $2 per overnight permit
was an appropriate amount.   SD   D   A   SA   NO

If you disagree, what do you suggest? _____

e. The information about
fees was adequate.   SD   D   A   SA   NO

If you disagree, how could the information be improved?

_____

f. The process of paying
fees was easy.   SD   D   A   SA   NO

If you disagree, how could the process be improved?

_____

g. The Boundary Waters is
better off due to these fees.   SD   D   A   SA   NO

RECENT EVENTS IN THE BOUNDARY WATERS

---

16. Are you aware of the extensive storm blowdown that occurred in the Boundary
    Waters in 1999? (Circle one response)

    1. Yes
    2. No → Go to question 19

17. Did the blowdown affect your plans to visit the Boundary Waters in past years (1999-2006)? (Circle one response)

    1. No
    2. Yes → If Yes, then how did the blowdown affect your plans?

_____
_____
_____
_____

18. Did the blowdown affect your plans to visit the Boundary Waters this year (2007)? (Circle one response)

    1. No
    2. Yes → If Yes, then how did the blowdown affect your plans?

_____
_____
_____
_____

19. Are you aware of the prescribed burning (management-ignited fires) that have been occurring in the Boundary Waters? (Circle one response)

    1. Yes
    2. No → Go to question 22

20. Did the prescribed burning (management-ignited fires) affect your plans to visit the Boundary Waters in past years (2000-2006)? (Circle one response)

    1. No
    2. Yes → If Yes, then how did the management-ignited fires affect your plans?

_____
_____
_____
_____

21. Did the prescribed burning (management-ignited fires) affect your plans to visit the Boundary Waters this year (2007)? (Circle one response)

    1. No
    2. Yes → If Yes, then how did the management-ignited fires affect your plans?

_____
_____
_____
_____

22. Are you aware of the lightning-ignited fires (Turtle Lake Fire and Cavity Lake Fire) that occurred in the Boundary Waters last year? (Circle one response)

    1.   Yes
    2.   No → Go to question 25

23. Did the lightning-ignited fires affect your plans to visit the Boundary Waters last year (2006)? (Circle one response)

    1.   No
    2.   Yes → If Yes, then how did the lightning-ignited fires affect your plans?

_____

_____

_____

_____

24. Did the lightning-ignited fires affect your plans to visit the Boundary Waters this year (2007)? (Circle one response)

    1.   No
    2.   Yes → If Yes, then how did the lightning-ignited fires affect your plans?

_____

_____

_____

_____

25. During this visit to the Boundary Waters

    a. Did you go into an area affected by the 1999 Blowdown?
        1. Yes   2. No   3. Unsure

    b. Did you go into an area affected by the prescribed burning?
        1. Yes   2. No   3. Unsure

    c. Did you go into an area affected by the 2006 lightning-ignited fires?
        1. Yes   2. No   3. Unsure

26. How important were each of the following factors in choosing <u>a specific area to visit this year?</u>

	Not Important	Somewhat Important	Very Important
Natural place, lack of human evidence	1	2	3
Remoteness, solitude	1	2	3
Scenic beauty	1	2	3
Easy access	1	2	3
Quality fishing	1	2	3
1999 Blowdown	1	2	3
Occurrence of prescribed burning	1	2	3
Occurrence of lightning-ignited fires	1	2	3
Test outdoor skills	1	2	3
Familiarity, been there before	1	2	3
A new area, variety	1	2	3
A friend or family member suggested it	1	2	3
Presence of good parking	1	2	3
Presence of pictographs/petroglyphs	1	2	3
Length of portages	1	2	3
Availability of permits	1	2	3

27. As you think about <u>any wilderness</u>, not just the Boundary Waters, how desirable or undesirable do you think each of the following things is? (Circle one scale response for each question)

	Very Undesirable	Undesirable	Neutral, neither Desirable nor Undesirable	Desirable	Very Desirable
a. Absence of human-made features, except trails and portages	VU	U	N	D	VD
b. Lakes behind small man-made dams	VU	U	N	D	VD
c. Leaving some areas without easy access	VU	U	N	D	VD
d. Bridges over creeks where you would otherwise get wet feet when portaging or hiking	VU	U	N	D	VD

27. Continued….

	Very Undesirable	Undesirable	Neutral, neither Desirable nor Undesirable	Desirable	Very Desirable
e. Designated campsites with permanent fire grates and pit toilets	VU	U	N	D	VD
f. Suppress fires that are started by lightning	VU	U	N	D	VD
g. Prohibiting wood fires where dead wood is scarce (requiring use of gas stoves)	VU	U	N	D	VD
h. Restricting the number of visitors to an area if it is being used beyond capacity	VU	U	N	D	VD
i. Accurate information on how you can travel and camp in the wilderness to reduce your impacts	VU	U	N	D	VD
j. Use of chain saws by the administrators to clear trails and portages of trees	VU	U	N	D	VD
k. Packing unburnable garbage back out of the wilderness	VU	U	N	D	VD
l. Evidence of natural disturbance (e.g., fire, blowdown, flooding, etc.)	VU	U	N	D	VD
m. Visitors using electronic GPS units for navigation	VU	U	N	D	VD
n. Visitors carrying cell or satellite phones	VU	U	N	D	VD
o. Use of prescribed burning to reduce the risk of escaped wildfires	VU	U	N	D	VD
p. Use of prescribed burning to restore the natural role of fire	VU	U	N	D	VD

USDA Forest Service Res. Pap. RMRS-RP-91. 2012

28. Your previous wilderness use:

a. How many times have you visited   _____ PREVIOUS VISITS
the Boundary Waters before this trip?

b. What year did you first visit   _____ YEAR
the Boundary Waters?

c. How many other federal Wilderness   ____ NONE
areas have you visited, besides the   ____ 1 – 2 OTHER AREAS
Boundary Waters?   ____ 3 – 5 OTHER AREAS
    ____ 6 – 10 OTHER AREAS
    ____ 11 – 20 OTHER AREAS
    ____ OVER 20 OTHER AREAS

d. What year did you first visit another   _____ YEAR
federal wilderness area, besides the
Boundary Waters?

e. Including this visit, how many times   _____ VISITS
did you visit a wilderness in the
past 12 months?   Is this number more or less than
for previous years?
1. MORE   2. LESS
WHY?_____
_____
_____

f. How many total days did you spend in
wilderness on all visits in the past   _____ DAYS
12 months
    Is this number more or less than
for previous years?
1. MORE   2. LESS
WHY?_____
_____
_____

29. Since you first visited a wilderness area, about how often have you gone on
wilderness trips? (Circle one number)

1. THIS WAS MY FIRST TRIP
2. TYPICALLY GO INTO WILDERNESS LESS THAN ONCE EVERY 2 YEARS
3. ABOUT 1 TRIP EVERY 2 YEARS
4. ABOUT 1 TRIP PER YEAR
5. 2 TO 10 TRIPS PER YEAR
6. MORE THAN 10 TRIPS PER YEAR

30. How often did your parents take you on the following kinds of camping trips (overnight trips)? (Circle one response for each kind of trip)

	Never	Occa-sionally	Often	Don't know
a. On hiking or canoe trips	0	1	2	DK
b. In auto campgrounds	0	1	2	DK

31. Do you belong to any environmental or outdoor recreation organizations? (Circle one response)   1. Yes   2. No

If yes, please list them:_____

_____

_____

32. In what type of community did you mostly **grow up** in before age 18, and in what type of community do you **now live**? (Circle one number in each column that best represents your past and current residences)

	Childhood Residence	Current Residence
• On an agricultural farm or ranch	1	1
• Rural nonagricultural	2	2
• Small town or village (under 1,000)	3	3
• Town, large village (1,000 to 5,000 population)	4	4
• Small city (5,000 to 50,000 people)	5	5
• Medium city (50,000 to 1 million population)	6	6
• Major city or metropolitan area (over 1 million)	7	7

33. What is the highest level of education you have attained? (Circle one number that best represents your education)

1. Less than a high school diploma
2. High school graduate or GED
3. Trade or professional school
4. Some college
5. Undergraduate college degree *(BS, BA, etc.)*
6. Some graduate school
7. Graduate degree *(MS, PhD, MD, JD, etc.)*

USDA Forest Service Res. Pap. RMRS-RP-91. 2012

34. If you are a student, are you: (Circle one response)

    1. Full Time
    2. Part Time

35. Are you: (Circle one)

    1. Female   2. Male

36. What was your age on your last birthday?

    _____ YEARS

37. Are you of Spanish, Hispanic, or Latino ethnic origin? (Circle one response)

    1. Yes   2. No

38. Select one or more of the following categories that best describe your race. (Check all that apply)

    ☐ White
    ☐ American Indian/Alaska Native
    ☐ Asian
    ☐ Black/ African American
    ☐ Native Hawaiian or other Pacific Islander
    ☐ Other

39. What was your annual household income in the year 2006, before taxes? (Circle one number that best represents your income)

    1. Less than $20,000   7. $120,000 to $139,999
    2. $20,000 to $39,999   8. $140,000 to $159,999
    3. $40,000 to $59,999   9. $160,000 to $179,999
    4. $60,000 to $79,999   10. $180,000 to $199,999
    5. $80,000 to $99,999   11. $200,000 or more
    6. $100,000 to $119,999

40. How many people were supported by this household income in the year 2006?

    _____ PEOPLE

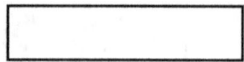

Public reporting burden for this collection of information is estimated to average 20 minutes per response, including the time for reviewing instructions, searching existing data sources, gathering and maintaining the data needed, and completing and reviewing the collection of information. Send comments regarding this burden estimate or any other aspect of this collection of information, including suggestions for reducing this burden to Department of Agriculture, Clearance Officer, OIRM, Room 404-W, Washington, DC 20250; and to the Office of Management and Budget, Paperwork Reduction Project (OMB#0596-0208), Washington, DC 20503.

Thank You!

PLEASE USE THE REMAINING SPACE TO MAKE ANY FURTHER COMMENTS

The Rocky Mountain Research Station develops scientific information and technology to improve management, protection, and use of the forests and rangelands. Research is designed to meet the needs of the National Forest managers, Federal and State agencies, public and private organizations, academic institutions, industry, and individuals. Studies accelerate solutions to problems involving ecosystems, range, forests, water, recreation, fire, resource inventory, land reclamation, community sustainability, forest engineering technology, multiple use economics, wildlife and fish habitat, and forest insects and diseases. Studies are conducted cooperatively, and applications may be found worldwide.

Station Headquarters
Rocky Mountain Research Station
240 W Prospect Road
Fort Collins, CO 80526
(970) 498-1100

Research Locations

Flagstaff, Arizona	Reno, Nevada
Fort Collins, Colorado	Albuquerque, New Mexico
Boise, Idaho	Rapid City, South Dakota
Moscow, Idaho	Logan, Utah
Bozeman, Montana	Ogden, Utah
Missoula, Montana	Provo, Utah

www.fs.fed.us/rmrs